THE NOR LOCH

The Nor' Loch

Scotland's Lost Loch

MALCOLM FIFE

© Malcolm Fife 2001, 2004

First published in 2001

This edition published in 2004
on behalf of the author by
Scotforth Books Ltd
Carnegie House
Chatsworth Road
Lancaster LA1 4SL

www.carnegiepublishing.com

British Library Catalogue-in-Publication data
A catalogue record for this book is available from the British Library

ISBN 1-904244-38-6

Typeset by Carnegie Publishing
Printed and bound by Alden Press, Oxford

To Sandy Crosbie,
Geographer

Contents

APPENDICES

Illustrations and Maps

Acknowledgements

THANK YOU to David Ross who typed the original manuscript. Also to Hamish Coghill, local historian. Caroline Wickham-Jones, archaeologist, and Ross Dimsey for checking the manuscript.

Credits

Sir Jack Stewart-Clark (Dundas Loch); The Rt Hon. The Earl of Morton (Kiershill Pond); Gavin Duff (Granton Gasworks Reservoir); Roy Drury, South Queensferry Library (South Queensferry Reservoir); Richard Gillanders, British Geological Survey (Prehistoric Lochs); East of Scotland Water (Edinburgh's Water Supply); Midlothian Ranger Service (Straiton Pond); Margaret Ann Stewart, Librarian, Heriot Watt University (Ponds at Heriot Watt); Sheriff David Smith (Curling Ponds and Nor Loch); R. Mowat, Royal Commission on the Ancient and Historical Monuments of Scotland (Lochend Loch); Dr Ian Tillett, Scotmalt (Humbie Reservoir and Pikes Pool).

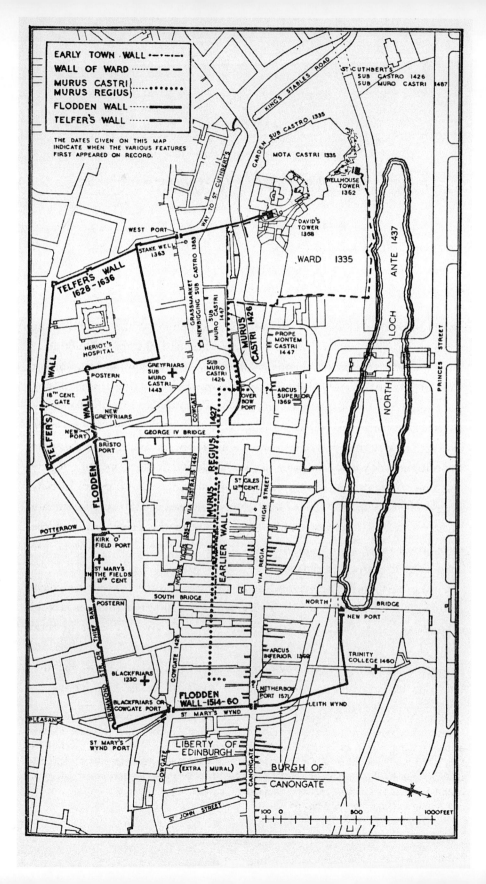

CHAPTER I

The Origin of the Nor Loch

A LTHOUGH SCOTLAND'S LOCHS are world famous, there is one loch that cannot be found on any recent map, namely the Nor Loch of Edinburgh. This loch, however, during its short life of perhaps around 600 years, was at the centre of numerous sieges and events in Scottish history. The Nor Loch owed its creation and demise to the hand of man, being an artificial body of water. Today man-made lochs are commonplace but a work of this type in medieval Scotland was somewhat unusual. For most of its existence the loch was in the ownership of the town. In 1603, King James VI expressly gave the Town Council the title to the lands, pools and marshes associated with the loch as well as the north and south banks. The loch, however, had been public property long before this date and although this body of water has since disappeared it is a fitting legacy that the valley it once occupied is now a public open space, namely Princes Street Gardens. The loch, when it existed, could have been said to have fulfilled a role of similar importance to the open spaces of the Burghmuir, being an important asset to the livelihood and leisure of the citizens of medieval Edinburgh.

Unlike many other towns and cities in Britain which have large rivers or other bodies of water in their city centres, Edinburgh today is devoid of such an asset other than the Water of Leith river. This is in total contrast to the area occupied by the city in prehistoric times. Then the land which lay between such rocky outcrops as the Castle rock and Arthur's Seat was under water or marshland. In addition to the city having an

Opposite: The Nor Loch and Medieval Town Walls. This map shows the position of the loch in relation to the modern street layout of Edinburgh. The North Bridge is close to where the dam across the Tummel river was and just beyond it Trinity College Church. At the other end of the loch is the Wellhouse Tower at the foot of the Castle rock. It should be noted that depiction of the boundaries of the loch varied greatly. A number of contemporary pictures show it extending almost as far as St Cuthbert's Church. (© *Crown Copyright. Royal Commission on the Ancient and Historical Monuments of Scotland.*)

artificial loch in the Middle Ages, several lochs formed at the end of the last Ice Age still survived. They included a large expanse of water at Corstorphine as well as Lochend and Duddingston Lochs which were very much more extensive than their surviving remnants today. French diplo-matic correspondence dating from around 1540 refers to Edinburgh by the name of L'Islebourg (islandtown). Use of this name continued until 1603 by which time the lochs around the town were in retreat due to natural silting and the digging of drainage ditches. Some historians suggest, however, that the name L'Islebourg had little connection with either islands or water. One theory is that it is a corruption of L'Aileburg (winged burgh) referring to the appearance of the site occupied by Edinburgh. Salisbury Crags were said to resemble the wings of a bird while the Castle rock was its head.

Initially it may seem rather puzzling as to why it was decided to form yet another sheet of water on the edge of the town. Castles are usually associated with moats, being man-made ditches filled with water to protect the outer walls. Many fortifications in Europe, however, utilised natural features to form a means of defence which included damming and diverting streams to form large areas of water in the vicinity of the building as a method of making the structure impregnable. It was also generally a far easier and more cost-effective method than having to dig an artificial moat. The original purpose of the loch was probably the defence of the town. Mention of this function is made in an act of council of August 1568: 'that when there appeared troubles to be made by the lords of the South and North and West Countries', the Council directed 'to big ane stane wall at the East end of the Nor Loch, cast fowssteiss' (build a stone wall, dig ditches).

The Nor Loch, according to many historians, was created around 1450 at the instruction of a military adviser to King James II. England was again menacing Scotland and another invasion appeared imminent. A small stream that flowed along the valley on the north side of the Castle and town was blocked by an earthen dam to form a body of water than became known as the Nor' Loch or North Loch. The English got no further than the Scottish border, being defeated at the Battle of Sark. The threat of invasion melted away but the Nor Loch was retained to become a permanent feature in the Edinburgh townscape for the next three centuries. W. Maitland, who wrote one of the first history books

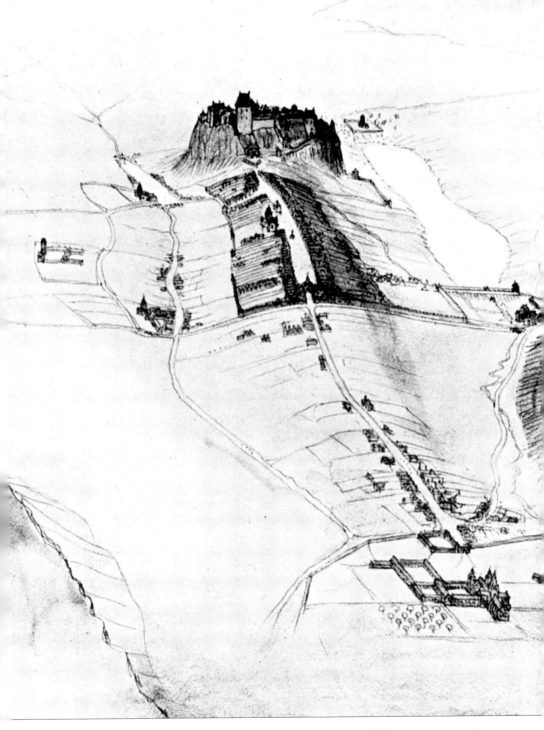

A bird's-eye view of how medieval Edinburgh may have looked around 1450. The town consists of little more than a single street which clings to a ridge bounded by the Castle and Holyrood Palace in the foreground. The Nor Loch can be seen to the right of the town. The River Tummel flows from it and passes Holyrood Palace. Much of the ground on the opposite side of the ridge consists of bogs and marsh. (*By courtesy of Edinburgh City Libraries.*)

on Edinburgh in 1753, was responsible for attributing the date of the formation of the Nor Loch as 1450. The defences of the town were strengthened in that year but the loch was already in existence by then. A document written in 1437 concerning the renting of an area of farmland on the north side of the High Street mentions access to the site being gained 'usque ad lacum' (to the lake), evidently the Nor Loch. This suggests, although not conclusively, that the waterline of the Nor Loch had not changed much since the early days of the Burgh which would push back the generally accepted date of its creation. There are no other references to the loch prior to this except for the fact that the Abbot of Inchcolm, Walter Bower, wrote in the fifteenth century that a tournament was held in 1398, on the site of the Nor Loch. King Robert III resided in Edinburgh Castle and Queen Annabella held this event involving twelve knights in which her eldest son Prince David participated. If this evidence can be believed the loch must have been formed between 1398 and 1437. The value of this statement by Walter Bower must be questioned as the usual site for the tournaments was at the west end of where the loch was, on a site known as the Barras. King's Stables Road stands close to this location today. This much-quoted reference as evidence that the valley was flooded after this date is in fact rather vague. All it states is that the event took place 'near to the north part of the town of Edinburgh, where there is a now a lake', 'ubi nune est lacus'. Although it fits the description of the Nor Loch, there were also many other bodies of water around Edinburgh in the Middle Ages. Another possible twist on this description is that the western edge of the Nor Loch often dried out in the summer or when the sluice at the dam was not properly maintained. Hence the tournament could have taken place when the Nor Loch was already in existence on ground from which the water level had temporarily receded and then maybe reclaimed by it at a later date. This could then also explain the statement 'where there is now a lake'. If this was the case the loch could have pre-dated 1398, and may have had its origins in an earlier century.

The Nor Loch is always said to have orginated as an instrument of defence for the town of Edinburgh. There is, however, no documented proof of this if Maitland's theory is discounted. More than likely it did first exist as a means of protection for the town which appears not to have had any stone wall on most of its northern edge in the early Middle

Ages. The slope down to the valley floor (where Princes Street Gardens are now) from the High Street was very much steeper then than today and possibly acted as a means of defence for the town, hence the lack of fortifications on this side. Over the centuries the townsfolk dumped their rubbish down the side of this slope which resulted in a transformation of the shape of the valley. In 1871, when construction work was taking place in Jeffrey Street, there was found to be a huge mass of 'travelled soil' extending downwards to a depth of about 31 feet (10m). All manner of ancient refuse – ox bones, cannonballs, old coins – many dating from Queen Mary's time – was found among the debris, as well as bits of iron chains and a great quantity of fragments of iron gear used for some unknown purpose. Incidentally this site was close to where the dam at the head of the Nor Loch was once situated. As the valley seems to have been a favourite site for the dumping of all forms of waste since time immemorial, there is a possibility that the body of water in it which eventually became the Nor Loch was formed accidentally. The stream that flowed through the valley could have become blocked as a result of the waste and debris deposited in the valley, causing a loch to form. The value of such a feature may have been realised by the citizens of Edinburgh who perhaps then built a proper dam across the valley.

The dam was beyond the protection of Edinburgh Castle which made it vulnerable to attacks and casts some doubt on the defensive function of the loch. When the town and Castle were under siege the dam for the loch could be easily breached. It has also been suggested that the dam was not created by man but was a natural feature known as a sill, a thin strip of volcanic rock. Such a barrier would be very difficult to destroy and there is little evidence that the dam was anything other than a man-made structure. A body of water like the Nor Loch would however be fairly useful in acting as a deterrent for undesirables entering the confines of the town even if it was vulnerable to attack from marauding armies. Some sources speculate that Dingwall Castle, which stood at the north end of the dam close to Calton Hill, served as a means of defence for it. The Castle, however, appears to have not been constructed until the early sixteenth century and used as a residence of the Provost of the Trinity College Church which stood close by. Another enigma associated with the origins of the loch is why Trinity College church was constructed a short distance in front of the dam at the head of the Nor Loch. It was not built until around 1460, many years after the formation of the loch. When the dam was breached the grounds of the church were prone to flooding. The site on which it was built on appears also to have been used as a rubbish dump prior to its construction.

The Nor Loch probably owes its name to the fact that on the southern edge of the town there was a loch called the South Loch. The original South Loch probably existed on the opposite side of the ridge occupied by the early town of Edinburgh. Its waters lapped over the site of the thoroughfare now known as the Cowgate. The loch, which may have been little more than a marsh, was drained in the fifteenth century. One of the tributaries of the River Tummel flowed through this damp depression before joining the main river in the locus of Abbeyhill. Perhaps it too was dammed to form part of the town's defences and complement the Nor Loch in this role. Unfortunately little else is known about this body of water and its name, the South Loch, was later transferred to the Burgh Loch, also on the southern outskirts of medieval Edinburgh. The Nor Loch was appropriately on the northern margin of the medieval town of Edinburgh. In most recent books and articles which mention the loch it is referred to in its abbreviated form, the Nor' Loch. Early sources, dating from the sixteenth century, refer to it, however, as the North Loch. Most official records and maps continue to refer to it as the North Loch until the nineteenth century. There is, however, a small number of references, using the shortened form 'The Nor Loch' in the seventeenth century which indicates that this use of the name is not a recent innovation. Perhaps the citizens of Edinburgh adopted the abbreviated form of the name in their conversation from an early date.

The valley in which the Nor Loch was formed was the product of the last Ice Age. The glaciers had their progress blocked by the Castle rock and gradually edged their way round either side of it. As they advanced they scooped out a fairly deep valley on the north side which would have only been revealed when the ice sheet began to melt around 15,000 years ago. It is very likely that the Castle rock was very much higher before the glaciers began their work on it.

As the glaciers melted they formed the many natural lochs that were to be found in the vicinity of Edinburgh in the Middle Ages. Although early accounts suggest that the Nor Loch was the first loch at this site, this is almost certainly incorrect. Evidence from soil samples point to the fact that there was a loch in this valley in prehistoric times.

Deposits excavated in 1870 when Waverley Station was being extended contained abundant masses of lacustrine shells, the majority of them unbroken. This is evidence of a loch bottom laid down in prehistoric times long before the valley was dammed.

Later deposits from the Nor Loch were found on top of this deposit in the form of brown earthy mud. Peat and alluvial deposits going down 80 feet (25m) have been discovered when boreholes have been made in the valley floor, which is evidence of a body of water being on this site for a considerable period of geological time and not just a few short centuries. Alluvial deposits in fact extend around the base of the Castle rock in a horseshoe shape. Hence in prehistoric times a body of water may have surrounded the rock on three sides extending from the site of Princes Street Gardens via King's Stables road on the west round to the Grassmarket in the southern edge.

It also should be mentioned that in prehistoric times, sea levels were very much higher than they are today. The sea lapped round the foot of Calton Hill at Abbeyhill, and may perhaps have extended some distance up the valley of the Nor Loch. Thus the site has seen numerous lochs and ponds come and go during its geological history. Going much further back in time to 340 million years ago, during the Carboniferous period, mud, marl and sand were deposited on the site of central Edinburgh from lakes and rivers. Fish lived in these lakes and their fossil remains can be found in Lothian today.

The Nor Loch was formed by damming the Craig Burn (some sources refer to it as a tributary of Tummel or Tumble river, its original name), close to where the North Bridge stands today. The latter names may be derived from the word 'timuil' which means 'dark', perhaps due to the fact that it flowed over peaty ground that would give it this characteristic. Although many nineteenth-century maps show it as a river, it was little more than a large stream being only 4 miles (7 km) in length. Its source was close to Atholl Crescent, near Princes Street, from where it flowed east to the sea via Restalrig and Craigentinny. Some Victorian historians said that a Roman road ran along the valley. It is claimed that evidence of this was found in 1822 when a drain was being dug in the former bed of the Nor Loch at the base of the Castle rock. Another portion of the

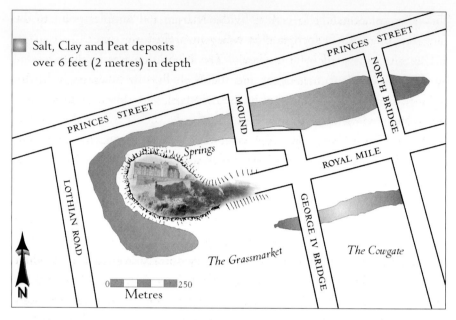

Salt, Clay and Peat deposits
over 6 feet (2 metres) in depth

PRINCES STREET

NORTH BRIDGE

PRINCES STREET

MOUND

Springs

ROYAL MILE

LOTHIAN ROAD

GEORGE IV BRIDGE

The Grassmarket

The Cowgate

0   250
Metres

N

This plan of the Castle rock and central Edinburgh illustrates the position of alluvial deposits. The presence of silt, clay and peat deposits around the base of the Castle rock is evidence that after the end of the last Ice Age there was probably a natural loch on this site. If it survived as long as the Iron Age it would have enhanced the security of the Castle rock for its early inhabitants.

alleged Roman road, composed of irregular rounded stones, closely rammed together on a bed of forced soil, was discovered when Trinity College Church was demolished in 1845. If this evidence is believed the valley which contained the Nor Loch must have been relatively dry by Roman times, if it contained a road that is thought to have linked the bases of Inveresk and Cramond. Modern archaeologists generally have tended to scorn this evidence and say the roads built in the vicinity of Edinburgh by the Romans remain undiscovered to date. A cobbled surface with Roman pottery, however, was discovered during recent excavations of Edinburgh Castle and appears similar in description to the nineteenth-century discoveries.

Being an artificial body of water, the level of the Nor Loch could be regulated by the opening and closing of a sluice in the dam. The loch was fed by springs issuing from Castle rock including those at the Wellhouse Tower which may have existed before the Nor Loch was formed. There was a further spring near St Cuthbert's Church and a short distance away was the original St Margaret's Well. Although the Wellhouse

Tower is sometimes referred to as St Margaret's Well, this is almost certainly an error. The original St Margaret's Well appears to have been on the north-west side of the Castle. The Nor Loch was further swelled by water from the Grassmarket and the West Port at Portsburgh. In the eighteenth century, Edinburgh historian Maitland said that there were two springs or wells issuing out of the Castle rock (presumably at the Wellhouse Tower) with some springs in the ground to the north. According to him there was only a small stream flowing through the valley before the loch was formed.

It is interesting to note that the Castle, despite being surrounded by a loch and springs, often suffered from a severe shortage of water during sieges. The rock on which it was built was basalt which has poor qualities as an aquifer. Water would tend to run very quickly over such rock when it rained, rapidly swelling the springs that fed the Nor Loch but of little long-term advantage to the garrison perched on top of the rock. The well on top of the Castle would tend to dry up in periods of dry weather. When the Castle was not under attack the water supply could be enhanced by using the springs at the foot of the rock. The Nor Loch itself does not seem to have ever been used as a source of drinking water by the local inhabitants, other than for quenching the thirst of their animals.

The exact origins of the loch are lost in the mists of time, and the traditional explanations for the formation of the Nor Loch are open to question. The date of its formation as 1450 is certainly wrong and the loch could date back a lot further than most sources give credit for.

CHAPTER II

Edinburgh Castle and the Nor Loch

THE NOR LOCH appears to have been created primarily as a means of protection for the town of Edinburgh but it also enhanced the defences of the Castle rock. By the early sixteenth century the traditional means of defence such as curtain walls, large towers and moats were beginning to look dated as the use of gunpowder and cannon became widespread. In some Renaissance fortifications water was used extensively as a means to distance the town or castle from the besiegers' cannons but this usually required the extensive construction of ditches and defensive bastions.

The Nor Loch, at times little more than a shallow pond, did not have the breadth to offer an adequate means of defence against the increasingly powerful cannon that were being built. Fortifications in Scotland generally failed to adapt to this new form of warfare until 1574.

Although Edinburgh faced another English invasion in 1513, it was halted at the border by the Battle of Flodden. In 1544 Edinburgh was not so lucky, with the town and many of the surrounding settlements being burned by the English. The loch appears to have offered little protection to the town on this occasion. A few decades later in 1573 the English were rather ironically asked to assist with the siege of the Castle. This became one of the most vicious assaults on Edinburgh Castle in its entire history.

The Provost of Edinburgh and Governor of the Castle, Sir William Kirkcaldy of Grange, held the Castle for Mary Queen of Scots after she had been forced to flee to England. An incident that took place in December 1570 had irrevocably alienated him from his erstwhile Protestant associates. John Kirkcaldy, Grange's cousin, was attacked in Dunfermline by the Dury brothers and their servant Henry Seaton. His

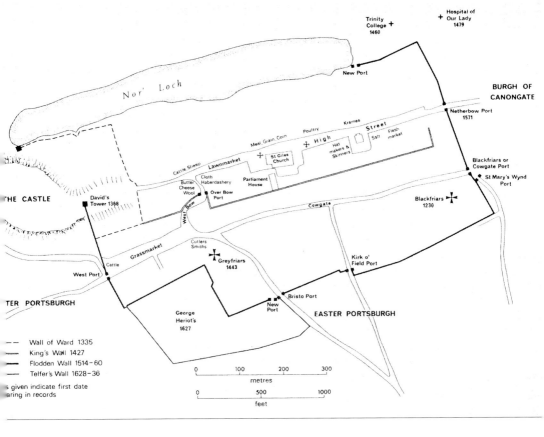

Trinity College + 1460
Hospital of + Our Lady 1479
New Port
BURGH OF CANONGATE
Nor' Loch
Netherbow Port 1571
Krames
Poultry
Street
Meal, Grain, Corn
High
Hat makers & Skinners
Flesh market
Salt
St Giles Church
Cattle Sheep
Lawnmarket
Blackfriars or Cowgate Port
St Mary's Wynd Port
Cloth Haberdashery
Butter Cheese Wool
Parliament House
Over Bow Port
West Bow
THE CASTLE
David's Tower 1368
Cowgate
Blackfriars 1230
Cutlers Smiths
Greyfriars 1443
Kirk o' Field Port
Grassmarket
Cattle
West Port
TER PORTSBURGH
George Heriot's 1627
New Port
Bristo Port
EASTER PORTSBURGH

- - - Wall of Ward 1335
King's Wall 1427
Flodden Wall 1514-60
Telfer's Wall 1628-36
s given indicate first date
aring in records

0   100   200   300
metres

0   500   1000
feet

Medieval Edinburgh and its defences. This plan shows that while the southern edge of the city was protected by a series of walls, the Nor Loch provided the main form of defence on the opposite side of the ridge. The wall of the ward was built in 1335 to protect the Castle. Some historians suggest the Nor Loch may have been created around the same time as part of this scheme to bolster the defences of Edinburgh Castle. (*From* The Making of Urban Scotland *by Ian Adams, by courtesy of Routledge.*)

life was only saved because of the intervention of the provost. A couple of weeks later Sir William sent six of his servants to take revenge on Henry Seaton. He was cornered by them on the harbour at Leith where a sword fight took place and Henry Seaton was killed. Sir William Kirkcaldy of Grange was then declared a murderer and throat-cutter by the preacher John Knox for this action. The six servants who had carried out the slaying fled from Leith and back to their master in Edinburgh Castle. While crossing the frozen Nor Loch to reach it, one of them, James Fleming was caught and imprisoned in the Edinburgh Tolbooth. His loss of freedom did not last long as Sir William mounted a rescue mission under cover of darkness. John Fleming was soon back in Edinburgh Castle along with his liberators.

The siege of Edinburgh Castle began in earnest in 1572 by Regent Lennox who was ruling in the name of her infant James VI. The Castle was surrounded by extensive siege works consisting of artillery and trenches, not unlike a First World War battlefield. During this siege the bombardment by cannonballs was not the only danger faced by the defenders. In the beginning of the month of January 1573, the besiegers had noticed that soldiers of the garrison were carrying water up from the Wellhouse Tower showing evidence of a shortage of water in the Fore Well. To prevent access to the well a strong guard was established by Regent Morton in front of the spur on the east side of the Castle and also at St Cuthbert's Church to the west. A counter attack was launched by the garrison in the Castle, who suddenly descended down the rocky slopes and slaughtered the soldiers in St Cuthbert's Church, leaving the building on fire. Perhaps this was a sign of desperation of the defenders for their need of water that they mounted such an attack. A week later, however, Captain Mitchell, with a strong force of soldiers from Dundee, arrived and reoccupied the ruins of the Church. According to Killigrew, the English ambassador, orders were thereupon issued to poison the well with white arsenic and new limestones and to fill it up

Edinburgh Castle under siege in 1573 by English artillery. Picture shows a battery on the site of Princes Street with the Nor Loch in between it and the Castle. By the late John McKay (*Copyright sought but unobtained.*)

with the carcasses of animals. It appears that eventually only wheat and lime were used. Numerous persons in Edinburgh Castle were said to have become sick as a consequence of the contamination of the water supply. The use of poison was soon found unnecessary. On the arrival of English reinforcements under Marshal Drury on 25 April, the Well-house Tower was effectively surrounded by the besiegers and this source of water lost ot the garrison. To further deprive the garrison of fresh water all the ditches in the vicinity of the castle were drained. The trench works of the besiegers also surrounded the water on the south-east side of Edinburgh, presumably the Burgh Loch. The Castle did not fall until the arrival of engineers and heavy siege cannon from England who disembarked at Leith in April 1573. Then the cannon were mounted on their carriages and taken to Holyrood to await the completion of the trenches and gun platforms. The English had supplied a cannon royal, six double cannons, and fourteen long range cast bronze guns as well as some mortars and smaller cannon. Edinburgh castle was by no means defenceless, boasting over forty cannon including Mons Meg. By a strange twist of fate some of the guns used to demolish Edinburgh Castle by the English had been captured from the Scots half a century before at the Battle of Flodden in 1513. Thirty-two cannon encircled the rock and blasted the Castle for six days. One of the batteries was positioned at a site where Frederick Street and George Street meet today. These guns were on the opposite shore of the Nor Loch, which provided little protection from their bombardment. During the attack much of the medieval Castle was destroyed. Today's structure owes its appearance almost entirely to buildings constructed after 1573. The tower built by David II, which was the tallest structure in the Castle, eventually collapsed after continual bombardment. It is said that large sections of it along with some of the defenders plunged around 200 feet (60m) into the Nor Loch when it disintegrated. The Constable's Tower which overshadowed the loch was also extensively damaged and parts of it must have also fallen into the waters below. One source said of the Castle rock that it resembled a 'sandy brae' after the siege, because of the pieces of rubble and masonry that ran down its slopes. The Wellhouse Tower was also a possible target as many fragments of bomb shells were dug up around it in the nineteenth century. A 48-pound ball was discovered in a breach in the Tower, its position indicating that it had been fired from a battery

The Nor Loch and Edinburgh, drawn by Captain John Slezer around 1693. This is the view that would have been seen by someone looking east from where the junction of Lothian Road and Princes Street is today. St Cuthbert's Church is visible in the foreground. At the far end of the loch the dam is just visible as are the towers of Dingwall Castle. A person in a rowing boat can be seen close to St Cuthbert's Church. (*By courtesy of Edinburgh City Libraries.*)

on the opposite bank of the Nor Loch. Another consequence of the collapse of David's Tower was the blockage of the well on the Castle rock itself, which hastened an end to the siege. It seems very likely that the loch was drained by the attackers, maybe by opening the sluice gate. Evidence of this comes from the Burgh Records which mentioned the damming of the loch in November 1573, a few months after the Castle had succumbed to the efforts of the besiegers.

The Castle was rebuilt after the siege and began to take on its present-day appearance. It was besieged several times during the Civil War in the seventeenth century. In 1640 it came under attack from General Alexander Leslie, Commander-in-Chief of the Covenanting Army. A gun battery 'mounting seven guns, large but of no great burden' was positioned on the north side of the Nor Loch. A further gun was placed at St Cuthbert's Church. This Church and its surrounding walls were a favourite venue for besiegers of the Castle because there were few other buildings around the Nor Loch to offer shelter from missiles fired from Edinburgh Castle. At this point the Nor Loch did not form a defensive barrier either, as it generally did not extend up the valley far enough to create a barrier between the Castle and the church. In 1648, after the Battle of Dunbar, the Castle was surrounded by Cromwell. A battery was placed near St Cuthbert's churchyard and his arsenal was near the site of the Ross Fountain in Princes Street Gardens. In many of the sieges following that of 1573, the batteries of cannon were placed in similar locations, possibly because the sites of that conflict were recorded in a sixteenth-century print that was published in Holinshed's chronicles. Hence there was usually a battery located on the bank of the Nor Loch opposite the Castle rock as in the siege of 1573. The siege by Cromwell is said to have been a rather half-hearted affair although considerable damage was done to the Castle and St Cuthbert's Church. His troops and horses were garrisoned inside St Cuthbert's. The result was 'the

It is believed the Nor Loch has its origins as a means of enhancing the defences of the town of Edinburgh. Although no traces of the loch remain, some sections of the town wall survive, such as the Telfer Wall built around 1618 and illustrated here. It is thought the first defences were constructed out of the turf and earth in the twelfth century when Edinburgh was given the status of a burgh by King David I. In time it was replaced by a stone wall which was rebuilt and extended as the centuries progressed and the town expanded. The northern side of the burgh relied for its defence on a deep valley and densely packed houses further up the slope. Some time between 1329 and 1437 the Nor Loch was created to enhance the defences on the northern edge of Edinburgh which never had the protection of a town wall.

church was altogider spoyled. Naither pulpit, laft, nor seat left therein and full of filth, and also the roof ruinous by shotts of cannone and muskett'!

The final siege in the seventeenth century took place in 1689. At times it almost became a comical affair and certainly lacked the intensity and savagery of the one that had taken place slightly more than a century beforehand. King James VII had fled to France and William of Orange was master of England. The Duke of Gordon retired into Edinburgh Castle determined to hold it for King James. The entire garrison consisted of no more than about a hundred and twenty men and four officers. One of the first actions of the besiegers was the draining of the Nor Loch in the belief that this would divert the springs from the wells in the Castle.

This shows that their knowledge of hydrology was somewhat limited as it was the springs from the Castle rock that fed the Nor Loch and not the other way round as they thought! Additionally a contemporary account states that the spring which supplied the Castle with water dried up due to the concussion on the rock caused by the firing of the cannon in Edinburgh Castle. Siege cannon were again positioned on the banks of the Nor Loch and at St Cuthbert's Church. On one occasion some of the attackers were seen cowering behind a wall in the churchyard. The defenders in the Castle fired several of their guns upon them making a breach in the wall, whereupon they fled leaving several dead and wounded. Another skirmish took place on the edge of the Nor Loch when a strong column of infantry crept up the north side of the Castlehill. This attack was repulsed by heavy fire from the defenders of the Castle who drove back the attackers to the edge of the loch. All the time they were firing their weapons the defenders were heard to sing 'the king shall enjoy his ain again'.

In St Cuthbert's Church records, the ministers often bemoan the fact that their place of worship had been damaged during the sieges. Sometimes the destruction was so great that their church could not be used for a long time after the conflict had been concluded. During the sixteenth century it had a thatched roof which made it very vulnerable in times of war. The gun battery set up by the English a short distance away in the siege of 1573 attracted gunfire from the Castle and the roof was set ablaze. In 1593 it was decided to erect a new church rather than restore it.

In the siege of 1689 the defenders made use of a secret route across the Nor Loch. The passage of the sally port (rear entrance) which they had been using initially was blocked up by the besiegers but the garrison employed an alternative route from the Castle gate and over the Nor Loch. It was operated in conjunction with sympathisers in the town. When any person was going to leave the safety of the Castle they were escorted by a party of six men commanded by a gentleman to take them across the loch. If someone was to be let into the Castle a sign was put in the house of Mrs Ann Smith (a grandchild of Dr Atkins, Lord Bishop of Galloway) and a party sent out to meet them. Once they were all safely back inside the Castle walls they let off a musket shot to signal the end of their sortie. Eventually the Duke of Gordon was forced to surrender Edinburgh Castle but he was well treated by the besiegers, as was his garrison.

In 1715 on the eve of the Earl of Mar's uprising, the magistrates who were organising the defence of the town of Edinburgh ordered the sluice gate to be shut to let the waters of the Nor Loch rise.

By the time of the second Jacobite Rebellion in 1745 this precaution seems to have been neglected when Bonnie Prince Charles was approaching the area. The loch's role as a means of defence appeared to be over.

In 1675 the Botanic Garden, or Physick Garden as it was known in those times, was established at the east of the Nor Loch, just beyond the dam. In those days its main function was to grow herbs for the medical profession, unlike the role of the Botanic Garden today. The area at the head of the loch was divided into six rectangular plots, three were on each side of the canal that acted as an outlet from the sluice gate at the Nor Loch. The plots on the north side of the canal were used to grow flowering plants. These three areas sloped from the north boundary wall to the central channel and therefore had an excellent southern exposure. The three plots on the south side were, however, unsuitable for this purpose as the area was overshadowed by the town wall. Like the rest of the gardens it had beds, walks and paths. The first of these – the fourth plot – lying to the north near a wall was organised as a place of instruction for medical students and plants used in medicine were arranged in beds in alphabetical order as in dispensaries. The fifth plot contained a small nursery while the sixth was planted as an arboretum with many kinds of trees and shrubs. Along the enclosing walls some of the rarer plants were grown under the protection of bell-shaped glasses and small frames. The walls were also covered with shrubs. In the late seventeenth century around two thousand plants were being grown in the Physick Garden. Like St Cuthbert's Church this enterprise suffered during the siege of 1689. Sir John Lanier and his commanders took it upon themselves to drain the Nor Loch as mentioned previously. The dam at the east end of the loch was broken to allow the water to escape through the channel that ran through the centre of the Garden. The channel was designed to hold only relatively small amounts of water escaping from the loch and was overwhelmed when the dam was breached. The Gardens were swamped with water as a consequence. When the pools dried up a thick layer of mud was left behind which resulted in most of the plants perishing. The head of the Physick Garden and his assistants spent many weeks rectifying the flood damage at considerable cost. He later received compensation for the destruction from the Town Council. In 1712 the keeper of the Gardens got a further sum of money to pay for the digging of two sewers for the draining of the ground. It is stated that it 'was much ruined with groundwater', perhaps seeping under the nearby dam.

Finally it is worth mentioning that there was one other castle in the vicinity of the Nor Loch, namely Dingwall Castle. It stood a short distance to the north-east of the dam at the head of the loch. The structure was probably not so much a castle but a fortified house with a quadrangular shape and towers at each corner. It was probably built for John Dingwall, who was the Provost of Trinity College Church, situated a short distance to the south, from 1525–32. He was a notorious philanderer who fathered a string of children despite being a leading member of Edinburgh's religious community. In the siege of Edinburgh Castle in 1572/73 it was used as a blockhouse by the forces attacking the Castle. It later served as a prison but by 1643 had fallen into disuse and was being used as a quarry for stone to repair other buildings. Waverley station now stands on its site.

CHAPTER III

Civil Disorder and the Nor Loch

THE PEACE OF THE Nor Loch waters was shattered not only by the firing of cannonballs from siege guns but by dissension among the citizens of Edinburgh, which resulted in several skirmishes.

In 1517 the country was divided in support between the Douglases of Angus and the Hamiltons. Edinburgh became the centre of friction among these two factions. Eventually the hostilities between the two groups resulted in open conflict in the streets of the town. In April 1520, the Earl of Arran and the chief adherents of the Hamilton faction assembled secretly to formulate a plan for the capture of the Earl of Angus and the overthrow of the Douglases. William Douglas got word of this scheme and stormed the Netherbow Port. The Hamiltons were routed, leaving around eighty of their supporters lying dead in the streets. Archbishop Beaton, who was on the losing side was forced to flee for his life and take sanctuary in Blackfriars Church. He was later captured by the Douglases and was found to be wearing a suit of armour under his robes. Some of the Hamiltons escaped slaughter by swimming their horses across the loch. The incident became known as 'Cleanse the Causeway', because the bemused onlookers were left to clean the streets of the bloody mess left after the skirmish. Their leader, the Earl of Arran, and his son escaped in this manner, mounted on a coal horse! Less fortunate was Sir Patrick Blackadder who was slain by the Douglases in 1526 while attempting to swim his charger across the loch to escape the enemy's lances and hagbuts (a muzzle-loaded gun of a type common throughout Scotland).

In 1558 there was another major disturbance on the streets of Edinburgh between the Catholic Church and the Reformers. The great statue of St Giles, the town's patron saint, was the natural centrepiece of the annual religious procession that was held on the first day of September. It was stolen by the Reformers less than two months before the parade was due

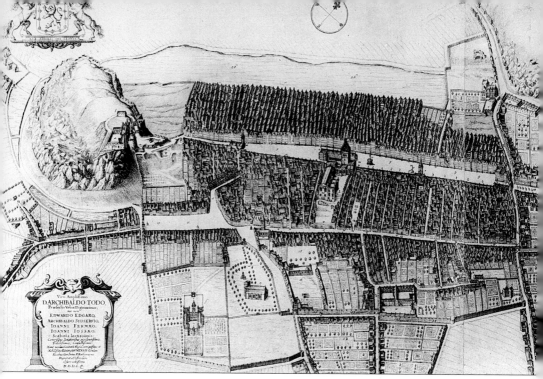

Bird's-eye view of Edinburgh in 1647 by James Gordon of Rothiemay. The Nor Loch is the prominent feature at the top of the plan. At the western end is the Castle and at the eastern side is Trinity College Church. Calton Hill is in the top right-hand corner. (*By courtesy of Edinburgh City Libraries*.)

to take place. They threw the statue into the Nor Loch. The Council eventually substituted a smaller statue for the parade from Greyfriars. On the actual day of the event a long procession of canons and priests with the Queen Regent at its head made its way along the High Street. Once the Royal representative left, a riot erupted on the streets and the members of the Catholic clergy had to flee for their lives. The borrowed statue was left in pieces on the ground. This was the last time St Giles Day Procession was held in Edinburgh. This disturbance was, according to John Knox, the natural climax of the anti-Catholic feeling in the Burgh.

When the reformers had 'excommunicated' the statue of St Giles to the waters of the loch they probably thought such an action would be symbolic. The waters of the loch were used to drown offenders against morality, especially those of the female sex.

In the 1820s when the Nor Loch valley was in the process of being transformed into Princes Street Gardens, the antiquarian James Skene, who was supervising the operation, stated that he had hoped to find the statue of St Giles in the mud on the valley floor. His search was in vain; perhaps because, according to some sources, the reformers who threw the effigy of the saint into the loch apparently had second thoughts about their action. It is said they recovered it a short time later from the water and committed it to flames. Maybe they thought that the saint could possibly be resurrected from the waters of the Nor Loch, while there was no chance of this happening if the effigy was burnt.

Mobs and rioters did not always have matters all their own way. Shortly after the accession of Charles I, the Provost of Edinburgh, who was unpopular with many of the townsfolk, was assaulted and had his house set on fire by rioters. When order was restored, several of the rioters were seized, including Andrew Gray who was the ringleader. The death sentence was passed on him and was scheduled to be carried out a short time later. The night before he was due to be executed he effected an escape from the Tolbooth where he had been held. A rope and a file had been smuggled into the prison by his friends. Once out of the confines of the prison Gray made his way down to the shores of the Nor Loch where a boat was waiting to meet him. By the following morning he was on board a vessel bound for France.

Years passed and in 1645, Edinburgh was in the grip of the plague. To add to the citizens' woes, an unusual sailing ship was anchored in the Firth of Forth within view of the Town. Experienced seamen identified it as an Algerian Rover. Expecting an attack by pirates, Edinburgh's provost offered to ransom the city to the captain of the ship. On hearing that the provost's daughter was stricken with the plague the leader of the Moorish pirates announced that he had the necessary potions and skills to effect a cure. His offer was accepted and a few days later the girl had been restored to full health. The Moorish leader then revealed his identity as Andrew Gray who had fled Edinburgh a decade before. After fleeing abroad he was captured by pirates and sold as a slave. He eventually obtained a post in the court of the ruler of Morocco. Here he rose to a top position in the household. Initially he returned to Edinburgh seeking revenge on those whom had imprisoned him, but he had a change of heart and eventually married the provost's daughter. They went on to live in a house referred to as Morocco Land in the Canongate a short distance from the Nor Loch, which he had escaped across many years earlier. There are, however, several different versions of this account, which casts some doubt on its authenticity, although recent research, has given this story more credibility. At the end of the twentieth century the wreck of a North African pirate vessel was discovered off the coast of south west England. Moorish pirates raided the coast of Europe between the sixteenth and eighteenth centuries with their activities peaking in the seventeenth century. Their ships ranged as far afield as Ireland and Iceland. Rather surprisingly it was not unknown for the Moorish vessels to be captained by Europeans, particularly from Britain or the Netherlands. Perhaps Andrew Gray was one of these mercenary seamen.

CHAPTER IV

The Nor Loch as a Place of Punishment for Witchcraft

ALTHOUGH THE NOR LOCH owes its existence to the requirements of defence it is better known for its associations as a place of punishment, particularly for witches and wizards. More witches are said to have been burnt at Edinburgh than in any other place in Scotland. The favourite site for their execution was on Castlehill overlooking the Nor Loch. Between 1479 and 1722, some sources state more than 4,000 men and women were sentenced to death for witchcraft in Scotland. One book, *Scottish Witches*, published in the late twentieth century, states the number of persons tortured and put to death as being over 17,000. A survey of Scottish witchcraft completed in 2003 by Edinburgh University, however, could only find documented cases of 3,837

people being accused of witchcraft between 1563 and 1736. These figures probably considerably underestimate the numbers accused of witchcraft as records would have only been kept in a certain number of cases and others will have been lost over the centuries. Around 1,000 persons in England suffered a similar fate despite the fact that Scotland's neighbour had around five times as many inhabitants. The Castlehill is said to have witnessed over 300 of these executions. Today the site is marked by a plaque at the entrance to the Castle Esplanade. Before the person accused of being a witch was burnt they were subjected to a number of tests to prove their guilt. One of these involved the suspect being thrown into the waters of the Nor Loch. If they floated it was taken as positive proof that they were indeed in league with dark forces. Some recent studies of witchcraft in Scotland, however, have thrown doubt on the practice of the 'swimming of witches'. Their evidence is based on the study of surviving records of witchcraft trials. In theory torture was only to be used with the permission of the State. But it was frequently used without official permission to extract confessions from those accused of witchcraft, although there are few references to this practice in official sources. Perhaps the same applied to the 'water ordeal' for testing witches' guilt. There are a small number of contemporary accounts were persons actually witnessed witches undergoing the swimming test in the waters of the Nor Loch. Only those cases which appear in such descriptions have been included in the following pages. It is possible that many others were also tested for their guilt in this manner. In general the swimming test involved the alleged witch being stripped naked and bound in the shape of the Holy Cross. The victim's right thumb was tied to the left big toe and the left thumb tied the the right big toe. Often the suspect had ropes tied round

---

Opposite: At the entrance to the Esplanade of Edinburgh Castle is a small memorial that goes unnoticed by most visitors, namely the Witches' Fountain. It was erected in 1912 and commemorates the 300 witches who were tied at the stake, strangled and then burnt to ashes on Castlehill. While those convicted of witchcraft were usually strangled before being consumed by the flames, there were some cases in Scotland when the accused was burnt alive. This form of punishment was not only reserved for those convicted of practising the black arts. On the last day of February, 1539, two blackfriars, a priest and a gentleman were all burnt together on Castlehill on a charge of heresy, 'and it is melancholy to know that a King so good and so humane as James V was a spectator of this inhuman persecution for religion, and that he came all the way from Linlithgow Palace to witness it'.

The purpose of the witches' fountain is to record the fact that not all witches worked for evil ends. Notice the newly placed flowers at the bottom of the memorial.

THIS FOUNTAIN, DESIGNED BY JOHN DUNCAN, R.S.A.
IS NEAR THE SITE ON WHICH MANY WITCHES WERE
BURNED AT THE STAKE. THE WICKED HEAD AND SERENE
HEAD SIGNIFY THAT SOME USED THEIR EXCEPTIONAL
KNOWLEDGE FOR EVIL PURPOSES WHILE OTHERS WERE
MISUNDERSTOOD AND WISHED THEIR KIND NOTHING
BUT GOOD. THE SERPENT HAS THE DUAL SIGNIFICANCE
OF EVIL AND OF WISDOM. THE FOXGLOVE SPRAY FURTHER
EMPHASISES THE DUAL PURPOSE OF MANY COMMON OBJECTS

them so they could be pulled out of the water before they drowned. The victim was then taken onto the ridge of Castlehill and burnt at the stake. The accused was usually strangled before being consumed by the flames. The executioners were thought to be doing the victim a favour by liberating them from the clutches of the Devil by burning them! Such actions were believed to release the evil spirits in the victims. The swimming tests and other tortures for determining the guilt or innocence of the individual were often referred to as the 'worrying of witches'.

Surprisingly this activity of witch hunting, although mentioned in the reigns of James V and Mary, did not reach its zenith until James VI was on the throne. By then the Middle Ages had drawn to a close and the Renaissance was under way in Europe. The main reason for the apparent increase in superstition during the reign of James VI was the monarch's personal interest in such matters. His flatterers referred to him as 'The Hammer of Witches'. One of the lasting legacies of his interest in such matters is believed to be the appearance of the three witches in Shakespeare's play *Macbeth*. It is thought that to hold the King's attention, the playwright included the three witches at the beginning of the script for this would immediately pander to his tastes. James had in fact written a book on demonology which at the time was the accepted standard work on such matters. Anyone disagreeing with it would be accused of having dealings with Satan!

It is against this backdrop that many innocent victims met their end on Castlehill. Betty Arnot was a well-known character in the town of Edinburgh who had a reputation for her charitable work. Her interest in helping cure the sick was seen by some as having more sinister purposes. Despite her protestation of innocence she was tried as a witch at the beginning of the seventeenth century. A further four women were also accused at the same time of having intercourse with the Devil. All five women were sentenced to undergo trial by ordeal. Only Betty Arnot, however, was put to the test, while the remaining accused rather mysteriously had the charges against them dropped. It is has been suggested by some historians, not well disposed towards this monarch, that 'When the lubricant employed was the almighty dollar' King James would be prepared to drop his beliefs. His purse was said to be always open. It is possible that donations to the King enabled four women to escape having their guilt being tested in the waters of the loch. It should be noted, however, that when a woman was accused of witchcraft it did not mean that a death sentence was inevitable. In a study of 305 cases of trails of named individuals in Scotland only 205 of these resulted in executions, 52 were aquitted and the remainder banished or excommunicated. Many of those branded as witches fled to avoid prosecution. In the end it was only Betty Arnot, who had little money and no friends in high places, that stood alone accused of being a witch. She was taken down to the banks of the Nor Loch where she was thrown into the water with her thumbs and toes tied together. She sank below the surface of the loch never to be seen again, her innocence being 'proved'.

Another old and unfortunate woman called Elspeth Peat was seen to stretch out her hand and point in the direction of John Darrow's barn. With some imagination this could possibly be seen as her putting a curse on the farmer's building. More likely she was just suffering from some form of senile dementia. Elspeth was accused of being a witch and thrown into the waters of the loch, or 'dooked' as it was referred to in the language of the day. Unlike Betty Arnot, Elspeth remained on the surface of the Nor Loch. Air trapped in her clothes kept her afloat although the large crowd of onlookers obviously believed it was due to more sinister reasons. According to a contemporary witness 'shouts of horror rose from all around', 'Away wi hir, away wi hir; let her be worryit', were the cries that were heard. The mob was not to be disappointed, either, as she was promptly pulled out of the loch and taken to the top of Castlehill where she was burnt at the stake. The year was 1589.

In 1590, no fewer than seven persons were accused of being either witches or wizards. All of them were put through the ordeal of water in the Nor Loch and found guilty. They suffered the same fate as Elspeth Peat, being burnt on Castlehill. Their ashes were then scattered in the wind. This action was undertaken whenever witches were burnt as it was believed that if their body was not totally destroyed, Satan could have it resurrected after the execution. One of the seven victims of this execution was a Euphemia McCalzean, a young woman from a good family, who was said to be of great beauty. The charge against her was somewhat more imaginative than most under suspicion of witchcraft. It was alleged that she had whipped up a storm while in league with the Devil in an attempt to overwhelm the ship on which King James VI and his new queen, Anne Princess of Denmark, were sailing to Scotland. Euphemia was also accused of a number of less serious acts of witchcraft including the making of waxen pictures to be enchanted. Several other persons also came under suspicion of being involved in this conspiracy which became known as the North Berwick Witch Trials. Rather unusually Euphemia seems to have sealed her own fate by pretending to have been a witch by way of a practical joke. The authorities, however, took her claims seriously and had her committed to the waters of the loch along with the six other co-accused. When she was undergoing the trail by water, her lover from another well-known family, the Hepburns of Keith, tried unsuccessfully to rescue her from the Nor Loch. However, she must have floated as she was later taken to be burnt on Castlehill. During the following year nearly a hundred more persons were implicated in the plot to destroy King James IV by means of devilish sorcery. Over two hundred witches, both men and women, were said to have sailed to North Berwick in giant sieves to take part in a service in the church there. The Devil clad in black is claimed to have stood in the pulpit. Throughout 1592, many of those who were said to have taken part in the ill-fated North Berwick Sabbat were burned at the stake. A pall of heavy black smoke hung over the Castlehill and the Nor Loch accompanied by the stench of roasted flesh which was said to have nauseated even the executioners.

At the turn of the sixteenth century another unfortunate woman called Isabel Young was brought to the attention of the 'Hammer of the Witches'. She made the claim that God had chosen her to heal the diseases upon the earth. Unlike many other persons persecuted for being witches she apparently had a large number of supporters. Many of them were prepared to back her claims, stating that they had been healed by her. Those who claimed remarkable recoveries were probably suffering from imaginary illness in the first place and her role was little more than a faith healer.

Anyone outside the Church who claimed to be carrying out the work of God would incur the wrath of the clergy, particularly when their claims were apparently being seen to be true. They declared Isabel Young was discrediting God and King James instructed that she should be tried by the ordeal of water. The practice of dooking witches had the whole-hearted approval of King James VI who wrote favourably of 'the fleeting [floating] in the water'. It appears he said 'that God hath appointed that the water shall refuse to receive them in her bosom that have shaken off them the sacred water of baptism and wilfully refused to benefit thereof.' At her trial she defied her accusers to prove the charge and said, 'If ye call me a witch ye cast discredit on your Lord Himself, who has ordered me to heal His flock.' This was taken as an act of blasphemy but again Isabel had her answer ready: 'Nothing can be blasphemy that comes from the Lord's own lips.' Public excitement grew so great that James VI gave orders that the ordeal by water should be carried out. To the surprise of the onlookers on the shores of the loch she managed to crawl from the water after she had been thrown in. Unfortunately for Isabel Young this was not taken as a sign of innocence and she was dooked again in the loch. She disappeared under the waters but surfaced a short time later only to sink again. Not satisfied with this result the authorities threw her back into the water for a third time when she floated – their suspicions were confirmed and she was led up Castlehill to be burnt as a witch.

It was not only women who were under suspicion of being in league with Satan. There was another similar case involving James or John Reid, who like Isabel Young was involved in healing the sick. Unlike her he was actually a doctor by profession, who claimed to have effected many wonderful cures. This brought him much admiration from the citizens of Edinburgh. Many of his claims were probably fraudulent. It was claimed, however, that his success was due to his alliance with Satan. This was backed up with evidence from witnesses who said they had seen Doctor John Reid walking round the top of Salisbury Crags in the company of a fiery figure that held a red-hot iron trident in his hand. Another accusation was that he had learned his art from the Devil whom he had met with many times at Binnie Crags and Corstorphine. The Devil had appeared to him in the likeness of both a man and a horse. It was also said that he had flown through the air like a bird from the Pentland Hills to his house in Edinburgh. According to Reid's confession he had made an unholy pact with the Devil – his soul in exchange for magical knowledge. The Devil had then given him three pennies and had instructed him not only in the art of healing but also in secret methods whereby he could destroy his enemies. With such testimonies his fate was sealed. In 1603, when he was at first thrown into the Nor Loch, the outcome was rather inconclusive. His second immersion in the water produced the results his accusers were looking for. John Reid was 'visibly showne by ye hand of God to be an associate of the Devil' and was taken up Castlehill for execution. It is said after he had been burnt at the stake there was no trace of any of his body. The explanation for this fact was that the Devil had come for him in a fiery chariot!

Accusing a person of being a witch or wizard was a convenient way of removing someone a person had a grievance against. Such actions were not restricted to individuals as there is at least one case of the authorities using the charge of witchcraft to dispose of persons who might oppose them politically. Long after James VI, the 'Hammer of Witches', had passed away, alleged witches and wizards were still being executed on Castlehill, although not on the same scale as in the early years of the seventeenth century. In 1656 seven people were accused of conspiracy against the government of the day, known as the Commonwealth and headed by Oliver Cromwell. The seven accused were said to have sworn loyalty to the Black King. This was in fact not Satan but King Charles and by doing so they had denied the Lord, meaning Oliver Cromwell. Rather unfortunately those charged had been hoisted by their own petard. They were in fact carrying out political activities under the rather unfortunate cover of witchcraft. The authorities did not accept their defence that they had just been playing at it and had them punished under the witchcraft laws.

Five of the accused were drowned in the Nor Loch while the remaining two, who presumably survived the ordeal by water, were burnt at the stake. The sentences were carried out in front of a large number of spectators who voiced their alleged hatred for witches by prolonged hooting and yelling.

On 9 March, 1659 yet another drowning took place in the Nor Loch, when a young married woman was sentenced to be tried for witchcraft. Several other persons charged with being involved with the 'dark forces and the Evil One' survived their immersion in the water only to be burnt on Castlehill between 1660 and 1670. By the closing years of the century the obsession with witches and wizards seems to have waned. After about 1680 no one else appears to have been tested in the waters of the loch to prove their guilt or innocence of being a witch or wizard. Perhaps a more enlightened age had dawned over Edinburgh.

In Scotland there was a strong belief in fairies who were themselves closely associated with witches. Both these species of supernatural creatures were very different from those depicted in Victorian story books. Witches did not fly on broomsticks or gather in groups at a Sabbat. The magical operations that they performed fell mainly into the categories of healing and divination. Fairies, like witches, often wore clothes similar to everyday people of the time and lived in a similar form of society.

In 1576, Elizabeth Dunlop was the subject of a well-documented trial in Edinburgh, 'Ane lang time been repute a wise woman and notour witch was brocht to the triall at the loch.' Elizabeth seems in reality to have been gifted with a considerable amount of natural shrewdness, which enabled her to discover the culprits of several thefts and result in the restitution of the goods. She was likewise in the habit of collecting herbs which she freely distributed among the poor. More seriously she added that she had no such power but if someone came to her seeking help in such matters she asked for help from a certain Thomas Reid who immediately supplied her with the necessary answer. When questioned who this character was, Elizabeth Dunlop stated her mentor had died many years previously at the Battle of Pinkie in 1547. He appeared to her in the form of an elderly man dressed in grey with a black bonnet on his head and a white stick in his hand.

On one occasion when she and her husband were travelling between Edinburgh and Leith on business, they stopped on the banks of Restalrig Loch (now known as Lochend Loch). While tethering her horse 'thair come an cumpanye of rydaris by, that maid sic ane dynn as heaven and erd had gane togidder,' (there came a company of horsemen who made such a noise as it sounded as if heaven and earth had come together). The riders did not pause, however, but plunged straight into the waters of the loch. Thomas explained to her that they were the fairy folk returning to Middle Earth (the fairy kingdom). Although many people benefitted from Elizabeth Dunlop's witchcraft she was taken from her little house in the Lawnmarket and led down to the Nor Loch where in the presence of an immense multitude the trial with water was commenced. Unfortunately she floated and in consequence was doomed to be 'worryit at the stake' on the Castlehill.

More fortunate was Sir Godfrey McCulloch who, according to legend was rescued from execution by a fairy he had befriended at an earlier stage in his life. His ancestors had owned Cardoness Castle near Kirkcu-bright in south west Scotland. Local disputes had drained the family resources and in the early 1600s the estate was mortgaged, eventually being lost completely to John Gordon in 1628, head of a family the McCullochs

Castlehill (in foreground) and West Princes Street Gardens. In the time of the Nor Loch the wooded area in the valley floor was under water and beyond was open countryside. Few if any buildings would have been visible. It is likely that there would have been few flowers or trees on Castlehill contrasting with this late twentieth-century view. In fact for many it would have been a place of horror and terror as those accused of witchcraft were dragged down the slope in the foreground and then flung into the murky waters of the loch. If they survived this ordeal by managing to float on the surface, it would be seen as proof of their guilt. The unfortunate victims would then be burned at the stake on a site on Castlehill which overlooked the Nor Loch.

had long feuded with. The McCullochs, however, did not give up easily. In 1668 Alexander McCulloch dragged John Gordon's ailing widow out of her house and threw her onto a dung heap.

A few years later Sir Godfrey McCulloch was watching workmen from the window of his house construct a new sewer to the White Loch below. To his surprise a small elderly man with white hair and a beard suddenly appeared next to him. This figure was dressed in a curiously cut costume and appeared to be very angry. He explained to Sir Godfrey McCulloch that 'I am the King of the Brownies. For years my palace has been inside the very mound your scoundrels are, at this moment, ripping apart in order to build a sewer.' To appease this irate fairy, Sir Godfrey McCulloch halted the digging of the sewer and had it rerouted to avoid the mound. In his gratitude the Fairy King would use his magical powers to help the astonished landowner should he ever have need of them.

Sometime later Sir Godfrey McCulloch experienced a decline in his fortunes and was forced to move to a smaller house at Cardoness. While there he got involved in an argument with his family's old enemies, the Gordons. During a dispute concerning some cattle, Sir Godfrey shot his neighbour William Gordon in the thigh. He died a short time later from his wounds. The year was 1690. To escape justice Sir Godfrey initially fled to France. He later returned to Edinburgh but in 1697 was recognised while attending a church service. Sir Godfrey was promptly arrested and sentenced to be beheaded by the Maiden, the Scottish equivalent of the guillotine.

As was the case with many executions, a huge crowd gathered to watch the event. According to legend, they were treated to an unusual sight. An enormous white horse appeared to emerge from the Castle rock. It galloped across the Nor Loch and headed towards the site of the execution. On this animal was mounted a tiny old man with flowing white hair and a beard, clad in a suit of green.

The crowd believed they then saw Sir Godfrey climb onto the horse behind the old man and recross the loch before vanishing over the Castle rock. When the crowd turned their eyes back to the execution site, Sir Godfrey McCulloch was still there. Even when the Maiden had severed his head from his body it was believed by many in the town that 'it was not himself, it was just a kind of glamour' (supernatural event).

A short distance to the east of Castlehill lay the notorious Mary King's Close. In the twenty-first century its remains can still be viewed deep inside the City Chambers. Mary King's Close was a thriving street in seventeenth-century Edinburgh. The Nor Loch was a few hundred feet to the north of this thoroughfare, which was the scene of numerous supernatural happenings. Its residents claimed to have seen 'spectres and nameless terrors' including ghostly dogs and ghoulies. Thomas Coltheart and his wife moved to a house in Mary King's Close in 1685. During their stay they saw a ghostly dog, a cat and a whole room of weird little creatures 'dancing prettily'. Needless to say they vacated their new home a short time later never to return.

In recent times people have continued to see ghosts on the site of this close. They have included supernatural cattle and sheep. Perhaps they are the ghosts of the animals that were butchered in the slaughterhouses on the banks of Nor Loch, a stone's throw away.

In 1685 Professor George Sinclair of Glasgow University published a book called *Satan's Invisible World Discovered*. Although he had an interest in the supernatural he believed implicitly in the evil of witchcraft, a belief which was which was driven home in his book. Regarding the 'Apparitions seen in Mary King's Close' he put forward a rather unlikely explanation for the tales. According to him the ghosts were created by clouds of methane or 'marsh gas' which rose from the dank waters of the Nor Loch at the bottom of the close. One of Professor George Sinclair's professional specialities was the effect of 'damps and wildfire' in coalmines. His gas theory may not hold much credibility for devoted ghost followers but it is relevant to note that sightings of the spirits declined with the draining of the Nor Loch!

Even once the Nor Loch was drained its associations with the world of the supernatural was not completely severed. In 1832 proposals were put forward to convert the East Princes Street grounds into a highly ornamental garden. At this time the site where the head of the Nor Loch once was found were recorded as still being damp.

The great attraction for children in the proposed garden was to be a Moss House at the north-west corner. It was to have windows of coloured glass through which the viewer would be able to see pedestrians on Waverley Bridge and the North Bridge 'in the shade of green fairies, swart savages or blue devils, as his fancy inclines him ...'

Like the witches and apparitions that once haunted the banks of the Nor Loch, the Moss House remains an elusive creation as well. It does not appear on any map or plan of that age, but it is not known for certain that it was never built! The site is now occupied by East Princes Street Gardens.

CHAPTER V

The Nor Loch as a Place of Punishment for Crime

THE WATERS of the Nor Loch were not only used as a means of punishment for witchcraft but for all types of other offences, including those of a very trivial nature.

Unlike the witches, who were apparently thrown bodily into the loch, those accused of other crimes did at least have the privilege of being seated while suffering the humiliation of being immersed. The Burgh Records for 22 May 1562 express the Council's concern about 'the lack of discipline by fornicators' in Edinburgh. The situation was said to be getting worse and more blatant mainly through the lack of any punishment for this offence.

In order to combat this alarming state of affairs the councillors appointed Robert Glenn, John Spence and Adam Fullerton to select a suitable place on the Nor Loch for ducking offenders. They also ordained the Town Treasurer, Luke Wilson, to prepare and fund this punishment with all speed.

In 1565 the English punishment of the 'ducking stool' (or in Scots dialect 'dookin stool') was introduced. The apparatus was erected at the east end of the loch close to the dam near Halkerstons Wynd. This public way has long since disappeared with the southern end of the North Bridge now occupying its site. The instrument of punishment was made out of wood and was not unlike a see-saw, with the victim being placed on a stool at one end of the beam and a rope at the other to pull the stool in and out of the water. In 1567, many of the sanctions introduced by Edinburgh Town Council for 'the filthie vice of fornication' were adopted for a law covering the whole of Scotland. It was only on their third offence that those committing this sin were to be fined or imprisoned and then finally 'to be tane to the deipest and foullest pule, or water of the toune, or parochin, there to be thrise dowked, and theirafter banished the said toune or parochin for ever'.

In 1575 Thomas Tribe and Mary Rose were ducked in the loch for leading a loose life. The woman was placed on the ducking stool but her male friend was simply thrown into the water with a rope attached round his waist. He was then dragged along the banks of the loch, no doubt with the enthusiastic onlookers all too willing to lend assistance.

In 1609 two meal merchants, James Martin and William Hart, were suspected of cheating their customers by adulterating their produce and giving them short measures. They cheated the country people who brought their produce into town, and also their local customers by giving them light weight. They paid little attention to any complaints made by their customers. Eventually the citizens of Edinburgh decided to take matters into their own hands and surrounded their booth which was sacked one day in early spring. The merchants were then led down to the shores of the Nor Loch where a ropes were tied round their waists and the mob 'dookit thame thryse, there after bade thame goe in peis'. Legend relates that Martin had a little daughter who accompanied the mob, sobbing bitterly and imploring them not to hurt her father. Perhaps had she not been there the merchants would have suffered more severely.

Not all persons were so lucky as to survive their encounter with the waters of the loch. In 1535 a Protestant merchant, Alexander Cant, was murdered in his town house which was said to be the finest in Edinburgh. Alexander was killed by his wife Katherine and her mother, Alison Rough, who was also a merchant and had amassed a considerable fortune in property. A violent argument had broken out between Alexander Cant and his mother-in-law over property which resulted in him being struck down and killed by them. The culprits were arrested and condemned to death. Katherine's execution was postponed, as she was pregnant, and she took the opportunity to flee to England leaving her newly born child behind. Alison also escaped but was soon caught. The death sentence was carried out with her being drowned in the waters of the Nor Loch.

Death by drowning was a fairly common form of punishment used throughout Scotland and not just reserved for those practising witchcraft. It also had the advantage of being a low-cost method of executing a criminal.

In 1628 a man called Sinclair was accused of committing incest with his sisters. They all eventually confessed to members of the clergy who were responsible for investigating the case. The three of them were sentenced to death because of the serious nature of their crime. It is said the clergy had a change of heart where the younger sister was concerned and decided to commute the death penalty on her providing she subjected herself to severe discipline by the clergy. The brother and older sister were taken to the edge of the loch and placed in a large chest with holes drilled in it. Once locked in the chest the two unfortunate victims were pushed out into the centre of the loch with the water gradually entering it through the holes.

Two centuries later when the Nor Loch was being drained and

East Princes Street Gardens, Edinburgh. In the Middle Ages a person standing at the same site would have viewed a very different scene from that depicted here. Most of the area in the foreground would have been under water. There was an unobstructed view up the valley to the Castle as the Mound had not been constructed. The Castle was much smaller and concentrated on the part of the rock nearest the Old Town which is visible on the left. The slopes on the right gave way to a gentle incline on which crops were grown.

converted into West Princes Street Gardens the chest was discovered. It
was found a little way to the east of the Wellhouse Tower in the spring
of 1820, when workmen were digging a drain through the deposits of
mud left by the now extinct Nor Loch. The chest is recorded as being
made out of thick fir timbers but quickly fell to pieces when it was
examined. Inside this coffin, it is recorded by the antiquarian James
Skene, were not two but three skeletons. In the centre was the skeleton
of a tall man and on either side was that of a woman. Perhaps the clergy
went back on their word to spare the younger sister. Rather surprisingly
many nineteenth-century accounts of Edinburgh history refer to only
two bodies being found, although James Skene in his account on the
excavations of 1820 in Princes Street Gardens which he supervised in
person, definitely states three bodies were contained in the chest. He
also goes on to mention that the remains of the victims were taken to
the edge of the then marsh and buried. Presumably the bones of Sinclair
and his sisters could still lie somewhere within the boundaries of Princes
Street Gardens, although they may have been removed when the railway
was constructed about twenty years later. The punishment for Sinclair
and his sisters took this form as persons convicted of committing incest
could not be buried in a churchyard. Entombing them in a floating
coffin was a convenient way of punishing them and disposing of their
remains at the same time. Some seventeenth-century historians hint that
several other acts of capital punishment were carried out at the loch.
Unfortunately contemporary records shed very little further light on
these incidents. It is known, however, that in the times of the Commonwealth under Cromwell a citizen of Edinburgh was tried and convicted
of 'bestiality' and was put to death by being drowned in the loch. The
man's name is said to have been Low and he was said to be connected
with one of the Lords of the Court of Session.

   This was not the only gruesome discovery made by James Skene when
reclaiming the valley floor from the marsh that covered it. The uncoffined
bones of an infant were found on what was once the probable edge of
the Nor Loch. Skene states of the discovery, 'there was a period in our
history when the frequency of child murders was quite appalling and the
facility afforded for its concealment by the mingy state of the Nor Loch
rendered it the usual scene of these atrocities.' One such example is related
in the Tolbooth records for 1662, where people were imprisoned before

punishment was administered. Margaret Ramsay was found not guilty of the murder of her own child but confessed to concealing the body of her prematurely born or aborted offspring in the 'New Logh of Edr,' presumably the Nor Loch. (It is, however, unusual for the Nor Loch to be referred to by this name but it is evidence that it had been created after the other bodies of water around the town.) Margaret Ramsay did not escape unpunished, being sentenced to be publicly whipped through the High Street for attempting to conceal the birth.

By far and away the majority of persons punished for a wide range of offences received no more than a soaking in the waters of the Nor Loch. Towards the end of its history the waters of the Nor Loch became very polluted and perhaps some of those immersed in this unclean water may have eventually succumbed to various diseases caught from this source. In 1595 Jean Tait was ducked in the Nor Loch for speaking scandalous words about one of the ministers of Edinburgh. She apparently was not too keen on being acquainted with the waters of the loch as no less then six lawmen were each paid twelve Scots pennies to administer the dookin. Jean Tait was then obliged to refund this sum! It is also a good example of how this form of punishment came to be used for more and more trivial offences. Men could be dooked for being 'profane swearers'.

Two years later Kirsty Balcanqual and Maggie Dow were dooked for 'being of notour ill life'. After being dipped in the loch they were literally whipped out of town but not before Maggie had struck one of her tormentors on the nose! This is not the last heard of Maggie as about four years later in 1601 she is recorded as having been dooked in the loch four times. The punishment was for the offence of being found very drunk in James Telfer's cellar. It was not the only punitive action taken against Maggie as she was fed on bread and water for a month 'to reduce the rebellious Adam in her flesh'. The unfortunate woman was whipped out of town again. Perhaps she had learnt her lesson this time as nothing more is heard of Maggie. Even someone who swore a lot or a nagging wife could be ducked in the loch on the dookin stool. A woman called Dame Jarlies is recorded as being 'sae dour' that she did not do any household work for her husband. She would neither cook his meals, clean his house nor look after his clothing until her husband David was reduced to a state of the direst perplexity. It appears she would do nothing but scold all day long at him. For this she was dooked in the Nor Loch. As in Maggie's case the punishment was no deterrent as not long afterwards she was brought before the court for assaulting her husband in his sleep. For this offence Dame Jarlies was imprisoned in the Tolbooth where she was to have her unwifely conduct specially dealt with by a deputation of Edinburgh clergy.

It appears the waters of the Nor Loch were used as an instrument of punishment for offences not only committed in Edinburgh but from far away parts of Scotland as well. In January 1599 Grissel Matthew, servant to Aberdeen Burgess James Seaton, confessed without 'tortour nor yrnes', to stealing a strongbox from her master's house in Broadgate, Aberdeen. She was tried in Edinburgh, and after conviction, drowned in the Nor Loch and her meagre estate confiscated. William Calder, a porter who helped to carry the chest containing private papers from the house, was flogged through the capital's streets, and then exiled. Drowning was often a punishment reserved for female criminals as it was deemed to be a respectable method of execution!

One of the best-known incidents concerned a woman known as Betty Trot. She was a hawker who had a small stall in the Lawnmarket for odds and ends. This was not her only interest as she apparently acted as a spokeswoman for the other hawkers in Edinburgh and made no secret of her alleged influence over the then Provost David Aitkenhead along with other members of the Council by openly boasting about it. She was eventually to fall foul of authority when there was a fire in a house in the Lawnmarket, around 1635. Once the fire had been extinguished it was found that some items of jewellery had gone missing. Suspicion fell on Betty Trot who was searched. The stolen jewellery was found in her possession and the punishment meted out to her was that she was to be ducked in the Nor Loch four times. This was to be done as a lesson 'to ken the differ between what was her ain geare and ither folks'. Although this punishment seems to be very light, as in those days a person could be hanged for stealing a sheep, Betty appears to have been a very self-willed person and did not easily submit to her punishment. When she was about to be tied into the dookin stool by the hangman, who was apparently delegated to overseeing the administration of her punishment, Betty suddenly lashed out at him. He was knocked head over heels into the waters of the Nor Loch. Before he could regain his senses Betty fled the scene and ran to a boat moored on the shores of the loch. She then proceeded to make her way across the water. The onlookers, however, were not going to be deprived of their entertainment without a struggle and gave chase in two or three boats. One of the boats eventually caught up with the fugitive only to have some of its occupants disgorged into the water when Betty managed to tip their boat as they attempted to board her craft.

Despite all her efforts Betty was entrapped by her pursuers and apparently made a gesture of surrender. As soon as the town officers grasped hold of her, she threw all her weight onto one side of the boat capsizing it and immersing the occupants. When Betty and her captors reached the safety of the shore they decided that all concerned had sufficient dookings in the loch and to punish her no further!

A few years after this there occurred a rather pathetic scene. A young woman of great beauty was sentenced to be 'dookit' because she had broken the Seventh Commandment (Thou shall not commit adultery). At least the supposition was that she had done so because she obstinately refused to disclose any information with regard to the paternity of her child. Though every means was tried to induce her to confess she repeatedly declined and eventually lapsed into silence altogether. The only words she ever uttered were 'I have dune nae wrang'.

In such circumstances there was nothing for it but that the presiding baillie should order her to be 'dookit' as an obstinate offender. Though her cheeks went grey with terror at the prospect, she refused to say any more. In the presence of a large crowd the 'dookin' commenced. The unfortunate victim had been plunged beneath the surface of the Nor Loch when a man was seen rushing along its banks. He dashed into the midst of the crowd, pushing the 'town officers' into the water and clasping the dripping woman in his arms, cried 'Who dared to dook my wife?' The presiding baillie shouted in amazement, 'Who are you?' The man replied, 'I am William, Baron Stewart of Ochiltree.' It turned out that he had contracted a private marriage with the young lady who was a penniless orphan in the care of his father. That father had wished his son to marry an aristocratic heiress, disapproving of his relationship with the woman in the dooking stool. The son had been obliged to go abroad on public service but in order to prevent any attempt to force his love into a compulsory marriage to get rid of her, William Stewart married her but kept it secret until his return from overseas. Stewart, however, was delayed on the Continent and her condition having become apparent led to the poor woman's expulsion from her guardian's house.

She never breathed a word of the truth. Sometime later her guardian died suddenly, and her husband was summoned home. Although she was now Lady Stewart, she never spoke nor would she until her lips were unlocked by her husband's arrival. This event created a great sensation at the time and was commemorated in more than one ballad.

During the 1650s, when the monarchy had been abolished and the country was ruled by Cromwell, a strict regime was imposed on the citizens of Edinburgh and many cases of dookin occurred, mostly for swearing. In 1652 the Town Council passed a law that any person 'fund guiltie of anything that offences the Law of God, shall be dookit in the loch twa times frae the pillar and stule by the lochside'. One man, Thomas Greig, was dooked six times in the Nor Loch because he likened the Lord Protector Oliver Cromwell to 'anne bulle of Baushan'. A woman with the rather unusual name of Flora Flower underwent the same punishment for calling Captain Elijah Proudfoot 'a yammering stinkpot'.

The dooking of persons for criminal offences was common throughout the first part of the seventeenth century. Around 1663 a woman called Margaret Robb was accidently drowned while being ducked for a minor offence. This method of punishment was then halted by order of the authorities. The dookin or ducking stool was allowed to fall into decay and relegated to become a plaything for children. The beam and stool remained a feature on the shores of the loch for a further twenty years until they were removed around 1685.

In 1717, a horrible murder was committed close to the current site of Register House, on an area which was then just rough ground. The crime was perpetrated by a young man called Robert Irvine, sometimes incorrectly referred to as Thomas Hunter. He was a tutor of two boys, the sons of Mr Gordon of Ellon. In consequence of the children reporting some liberties they saw him take with their mother's maid, he conceived a plan to murder them. One day when he was leading them for a walk on a narrow country road close to where Register House stands today, he suddenly drew a clasp knife from his pocket and stabbed the eldest of the children in the heart. The other boy fled but the murderer pursued him and slew him. The slaughter was observed by numerous people walking on the banks of Castlehill. In the days before Princes Street Gardens this location served as a recreation area for the inhabitants of Edinburgh. The witnesses of the crime were near enough to see every action of the murderer and hear the cries of his victims, but were unable to go to their assistance as they were separated by the marshy valley floor which contained the remnants of the Nor Loch. Robert Irvine was caught a short time later. The Baron of Broughton hanged him after first cutting off his hands.

CHAPTER VI

The Nor Loch as a Place of Suicide

NOT ALL THE LIVES snuffed out by the waters of the Nor Loch were as a consequence of punishment. It is estimated that about 150 persons were drowned in the loch between the beginning of the sixteenth century and the mid-eighteenth century. Some of those included in this total were accidental drownings while others were deliberate suicides.

To 'tak a dook at the pot' was an expression used by the residents of Edinburgh in bygone times for attempting to commit suicide. It had its origins in the name given to the deepest part of the loch which was referred to as the Pot. This feature was situated at the head of the loch on the north-east side, close to where the former General Post Office building at Waterloo Place stands today. The depth of the Pot was said to be around 15 feet (5m). It is not very deep when compared with some of the natural lochs in Scotland which can be hundreds of feet deep. Much of the Nor Loch, however, appears to have been very shallow with a depth of only three or four feet and could be crossed by causeways. One of the legends in connection with suicides in the loch is of considerable antiquity. A young woman of noble birth, Lady Mary Boyde, was left by her lover, Earl William, who had gone on a pilgrimage. The family of the woman banished her to a little hut on the edge of the forest of Drumsheugh because she was unmarried and expecting a child. Lady Mary spent her time wandering by the side of the Nor Loch awaiting the return of Earl William. Her child was born after she had spent several months in the hut but it died of the cold and exposure. Lady Mary was in despair and ended her life by drowning herself in the Pot.

Earl William returned from his travels the following day only to learn of the death of Mary. Before he had gone on his pilgrimage he had given

East Princes Street Gardens. In the days of the Nor Loch this was the deepest part of the loch. The Old Town is visible on the left and the Castle in the distance. There were once quarries on the site of the now flower-covered slopes.

his friend a ring which was to be passed on to Mary's father stating that on his return he was to make her his wife. The friend proved treacherous as he did not deliver the ring. Earl William repaid his friend's treachery by killing him. William then entered a religious house and passed the rest of his life in prayer. The ballad 'The Bride's Burial' commemorates this story.

Another suicide of noble birth in the waters of the loch was that of Alexander Elphinstone, brother of Baron Coupar. He wished to marry the daughter of the Earl of Menteith but her family had more ambitious plans for her and had arranged for her to be engaged to Mackenzie of Kintail. Her prospective husband was an old widower, who apparently had not treated his previous wife too kindly. After trying to prevent the marriage, Alexander Elphinstone in desperation took his life by drowning himself in the Pot. The daughter of the Earl of Menteith refused to marry Mackenzie of Kintail and died three months later from a broken heart. Tradition has it that she cursed the Menteith family who eventually died out in 1694.

Several cases of suicide are recorded in the accounts for the Town of Edinburgh. Sometimes the authorities had to pay for the cost of recovering bodies from the loch, which it must be remembered belonged to the town. In the year of 1591/92 there is an entry for 'bringing forth' two women who were drowned in the loch. The cost of this was ten shillings. This may have been an accidental drowning as it took place in winter when there was probably ice on the water. Another entry leaves no doubt as to the cause of death. A convict called Thomas Doby is recorded as having drowned himself in the Nor Loch in the year of 1597/98. His body was denied a proper burial and instead was taken to be hanged on the gallows on the Burgh Muir under instructions given from the bailiff.

The town records of 1587 mention a council decree against the husband of Sibilla Dewar, instructing him not to come to the house of his wife or molest or trouble her at any time. Ten years later a Sibilla Dewar is recorded as having drowned herself in the Nor Loch, presumably the same unfortunate woman. Although many suicide attempts probably went unrecorded a small number of them have gone on to become part of Edinburgh's history. In 1695 James Edmonstone fell under suspicion of the murder of the Master of Rollo with an accomplice called Patrick Graham of Inchbraco. Both of the suspects were banished for life but James

Edmonston's body was discovered a couple of days after the trial had concluded. When the authorities found the body in the Nor Loch they concluded that every appearance pointed to the fact that the accused had intended to take his life.

Some suicide attempts were witnessed by the residents of old Edinburgh. A man who was a shoemaker by trade was seen walking out into the waters of the loch by a crowd of persons who called out to him to have a second thoughts about his actions. The commotion disturbed a resident in nearby James Court, in the Lawnmarket. He leant out of his window and is reputed to have yelled down to the anguished onlookers, 'What's all the noise about, canna ye e'en let the honest man gang tae the deil his ain gait?' This prompted an outburst of laughter among the crowd of onlookers and the drunken shoemaker abandoned his suicide attempt and quietly walked out of the water. Many of Edinburgh's shoemakers lived outside the town walls in a group of houses clustered around the Trinity College Church, a short distance away from the head of the Nor Loch.

Several other attempted suicides had comical outcomes. One concerned a woman who, like the shoemaker, walked into the waters of the Nor Loch intent on drowning herself. As she progressed she found that instead of being immersed by water she was floating on it. Her hooped skirt had filled with air and was acting as a lifebelt. This also may explain why so many persons suspected of witchcraft did not sink immediately, implicating their guilt. A further humiliation was experienced by this woman when her voluminous skirt was caught in a gust of wind. This resulted in her being blown bodily across the loch to the opposite shore. When in full sail she had quickly dispensed with any idea of wishing to die as she shrieked for help! A boat was launched to go to her rescue but she reached dry land at a point near Lochside Farm, on the northern side of the loch, before they could catch her.

Not all the incidents associated with persons wishing to draw their existence to a close had humorous outcomes like that of the woman mentioned above. One such case was that relating to Joan Anderson, a daughter of a well-known lawyer in the town of Edinburgh in the seventeenth century. He was a well-known Royalist and when Cromwell came to power he refused to change his allegiances. This resulted in him incurring numerous fines which drained away his wealth. Anderson was banned from practising law until he recognised Cromwell's government, known as the Commonwealth. To add to his problems Joan Anderson had fallen in love with the son of a high-ranking member of the Commonwealth. The latter magnanimously offered to purchase a house for Anderson if he relented his beliefs to allow his son to marry Joan. By this time Anderson's wife had become seriously ill and his daughter pleaded with him to accept the gesture. His staunch beliefs would not let him be open to any persuasion. His wife died a short time later and his daughter, crazed with grief, went down the slope to the Pot and deliberately threw herself in. The onlookers did not stand idly by but attempted to rescue her immediately. Their attempts were in vain as Joan Anderson died before they could retrieve her from the loch. Her father then decided to leave Edinburgh and go into voluntary exile. When the monarchy was restored relatives went to enquire for Anderson at The Hague, his chosen place of exile. It was found that he had died a few months beforehand. In 1665 David Hunter did 'droone himsel in the Nor Loch, forasmickle as being a common dyvour he was na abil to mete his promits' (he was a common debtor who could not keep his promises). Many years later, James Burns repeated the same action because he had been discovered in an act of 'glaring immorality'.

Those who survived attempted suicide in the Nor Loch were sometimes charged with the crime of attempted suicide or self-murder as it was known in those times. One such instance involved a young man who had fallen in love with the daughter of John Bell of Stanakilly. She, however, was to marry someone else and on her wedding day, the distraught young man threw himself into the Pot. Fortunately on this occasion he was pulled from the water while still alive. He was accused of 'self-murder' and his punishment for this sin was to be appropriately supervised by members of the clergy, George Jack of the Auld Kirk and Robert Henry of Greyfriars.

Not all suicide attempts were what they seemed to be at first sight. In 1707, Robert Balfour, eldest son of Lord Burleigh, rode into Inverkeithing on horseback with two or three attendants, and challenged Henry Stenhouse, a schoolmaster, to a duel. When the schoolmaster refused to take up his challenge Robert Balfour pulled out a pistol and shot him twice. The victim died a few days later from his wounds. The quarrel which resulted in Stenhouse's death was due to the fact that he had married the woman Robert Balfour had fallen in love with when he was abroad. Robert Balfour was eventually sentenced to be beheaded. The punishment was to take place three years after the crime in 1710 at Edinburgh Cross. However, he managed to escape from the Tolbooth but was captured at Leith. His second escape attempt met with more success. Shortly after breaking out of his cell dressed as a woman, the alarm was raised and his pursuers cornered him on the banks of the Nor Loch. With a cry of defiance he shouted out at them that he preferred death to spending any more time in prison. Robert Balfour then plunged into the infamous Pot. The pursuers scanned the waters but saw no sign of him surfacing in the failing light. It was assumed that he had gone the same way as so many others who had thrown themselves into the Pot. No body was ever found. Robert Balfour was a strong swimmer and got clean away!

CHAPTER VII

Smuggling and the Nor Loch

THE NOR LOCH proved relatively unsuccessful as a means of protecting Edinburgh and its Castle against full-scale military assault. However, it was deemed to be an effective means of countering smuggling into the town, although the evidence for its success in this role is not too strong either. The ingenuity of the smugglers often made short work of this obstacle. As the pastime of witch-hunting was in decline in the seventeenth century, that of smuggling was rapidly increasing. This was due in part to the fact that in the year of 1656, the Protectorate government ordered a careful examination to be made of Scots revenue and the numerous evasions of customs duties.

From 1625 to 1760, Edinburgh was a hotbed of smuggling activity. It was conveniently near the port of Leith so that cargoes of contraband goods could be run ashore near the Figgate Whins, at the mouth of the Figgate Burn. Portobello occupies the shoreline here today, but in those times it was a desolate area devoid of human habitation. Another location favoured by the smugglers for disembarking their cargoes was the Drum sands, near South Queensferry. Once their contraband was ashore, a horse and cart would convey it to the banks of the Nor Loch when opportunity allowed. In the dead of night many a case of wine or coil of tobacco was smuggled into the town up through the narrow closes and snugly concealed in cellars until a distribution could be made.

In May 1663 certain councillors of Edinburgh were appointed to view a passage made at the head of the Nor Loch by which 'wynes and strong waters' were carried at night into the town. It was suggested that a large ditch be dug across this route to impede the transport of illegal contraband. The Nor Loch itself provided an obstacle to the transport of such goods but was a mixed blessing to the Town Council. When they lowered its waters by opening the sluice gate the smugglers of 'strong waters' had their task made a lot simpler, being able to use numerous causeways across

The Prospect of the Castle and City of Edenborow from the North Loch.

The North Loch.

Edinburgh Castle and the Nor Loch from a drawing dated 1690. The Wellhouse Tower is visible at the base of the Castle rock. The Castle looks very different from that of today. Most of the buildings are clustered together at the eastern edge of the rock while much of the summit remains bare rock. Trinity College Church is visible at the head of the loch, on the left hand side of the picture. The spire of St Giles Church looms over the town of Edinburgh situated on the high ground overlooking the Nor Loch. Note there is almost a complete lack of trees in the landscape around the banks of the loch. (*By courtesy of Edinburgh City Libraries.*)

the bed of the loch. No sooner were instructions given to restore the water level of the loch to its maximum height, than the householders and property owners on the edge of the rising waters would complain about their buildings being flooded.

Even when the loch was almost overflowing with water, the smugglers could usually overcome this man-made hazard. They were well organised and resourceful. It is probably no coincidence either that many of the merchants' houses overlooked the Nor Loch. There were several underground passages which ran up from concealed cellars in old boathouses on the banks of the loch, emerging in the centre of the town. One of these passages was uncovered when George IV Bridge was being constructed. The route it followed was from the edge of the former loch to a cellar below Robert Gourley's house in Old Bank Close, long since demolished. Lady Stair's, Baxter's and Advocate's Closes were also popular routes for smugglers bringing their goods up from the foot of the valley.

One of the best-known incidents concerning smugglers revolved around Jock Ramage, who was a character of some notoriety. He had an awesome reputation, smuggling cargoes for about thirty years, from 1690 to 1720 without ever being caught. On a cold dark night in November, the smugglers, or 'Jinkers' as they preferred to be known, were waiting for a signal from their contacts in Edinburgh to give them the all-clear to cross the loch. Once they believed they had been given the signal, three heavily laden boats were pushed out into the loch and rowed towards the town. All appeared in order when they arrived on the opposite shore and hastily began unloading their cargoes. Suddenly, three men rather the worse for some alcoholic refreshments stumbled across the Jinkers. Worried that their secret would soon be spread throughout the town, Jock Ramage did some quick thinking and took one of the beakers of French brandy from his cargo. He then filled up three horns with this potent spirit, and the three unfortunate spectators were offered free drinks with a pistol being held to their heads to make sure there was no doubt as to what would happen if they declined his offer. It was not long before the spirit had the desired effect and all three passed out. The final touch to Jock Ramage's plan was to have the men carried to their own doorsteps. That way there would be no doubt that they had imagined all the events of the previous night, never having been near the Nor Loch.

In winter the loch often froze over, making the smugglers' task a lot easier. Often they could reach the town without even having to use boats as they could just walk over the ice. In 1685, the Burgh records contain details of a petition by Andrew Mertoun, a wine importer, for an abatement of his tack (rent) duty on account of his losses. The authorities allowed 5,000 marks off his first year's tack because his business had suffered as the Nor Loch was frozen for many months and great quantities of brandy and other spirits were brought into the town under the cover of darkness.

The Burgh records for 1691 give an insight to the punitive taxes levied on alcoholic beverages. Two merchants, John Duncan and Edward Majoribanks, who had the licence from the council to sell alcohol, had to pay £50 (Scots) upon a tun of French wine. Spanish, Rhenish and brandy wines imported and sold in Edinburgh had the imposition of £46 on each tun. There was a levy of 12 pennies upon the pint of beer and ale. On top of this there had been a recent Act of Parliament which had hiked up prices with the additional tax of £30 upon every tun of French and Rhenish wines and £100 upon every tun of Spanish wine, 4 shillings upon every pint of brandy, and 3 shillings upon every pint of foreign beer or ale imported into the town. Interestingly the precincts of Holyrood Abbey were exempt from the duties imposed by the council.

(A tun was a large cask for wine or beer wth a capacity of around 210 gallons/955 litres).

The level of smuggling greatly increased after the Act of Union in 1707, when additional taxes were put on Scotland. To add insult to injury many of the customs officers employed to enforce the regulations were English.

The state of public feeling manifested itself in the Porteous Riots. The novelist Sir Walter Scott had one of his characters in his book *The Heart of Midlothian* refer to the Nor Loch in the following terms: 'It enabled an honest man to fetch sae muckle as a bit anker o'brandy frae Leith to the Lawnmarket without being rubbit o' the very gudes he's bought and paid for, by a host o' idle English gaugers.' (It enabled an honest man to fetch ankers of brandy from Leith to the Lawnmarket without being robbed of the very goods he paid for by idle English Customs officers.) An anker was a liquid measure of about fifteen litres or four gallons used by smugglers for convenience of carriage on horseback.

West Princes Street Gardens. The people in the foreground are sitting in what was once the bottom of the loch. By the eighteenth century much of this area had become a marsh with the surviving part of the loch only occupying the area to the east of the Mound.

Throughout its life the Nor Loch had several causeways running across it. Towards the end of the seventeenth century the loch seems to have become shallower particularly at the western end. In 1702 a committee from the Town Council reported that they had visited the loch and were of the opinion that it was necessary to put a new door on the town gate at this location to prevent untaxed goods from being brought into Edinburgh. It is also recorded that the water was very shallow near the dam and to the west of the street leading to the New Port opposite the foot of Halkerston's Wynd.

In 1707 the Council recommended that the town wall at Leith Wynd, close to the head of the Nor Loch and on the south side of the Edinburgh Castle, be heightened as a deterrent to smugglers. In the minutes of the Town Council meeting for 19 March 1740 there is a further reference to the Nor Loch which stated that it was the only 'fence' to the Town on the north side. It laments the fact that it had been so drained that encroachments had been made to the land on its shores. The records conclude that the whole situation was of great prejudice to His Majesty's Customs and Excise and to the revenue of Edinburgh. The ready access through the shrunken waters of the loch allowed smugglers to import everything into the Town free from payment of imports or customs. To remedy this unsatisfactory state of affairs an order was made by the councillors to stop up the loch until the water reached its ancient boundaries. Thus in the eighteenth century the Nor Loch continued to survive as it was believed that it reduced smuggling and as a consequence boosted revenues for the town. Within a couple of decades of this action to restore the waters of the Nor Loch to their old levels, the valley was being drained as the old priorities had changed. Smuggling declined after the middle of the eighteenth century, so the loch's remaining function was becoming redundant. The expansion of Edinburgh took priority and the Nor Loch was seen as having no place in the vision of the new city.

CHAPTER VIII

The Economic Role
of the Nor~ Loch

ALTHOUGH THE NOR LOCH played a major role in the black economy of the life of Edinburgh, there were also numerous legal enterprises associated with it. For instance, its waters were a source of eels and fish and the loch is said to have swarmed with perch. The minister of St Cuthbert's Church could sometimes be seen fishing for his dinner in its waters. Although the loch has long since vanished the minister still retains the right to fish on it in the opening years of the twenty-first century. The Burgh Records from time to time make reference to the fishing rights granted for catching eels. One such example is for the year of 1598/99 which mentions the tack for the eel ark (eel trap) being let to Alexander Adamson at a cost of fifty marks for five years. He was refunded five marks in 1601 due to the letting out of water from the Nor Loch during that year. The eel ark apparently was located not in the Nor Loch itself, but in the drain that was on the opposite side of the earthen dam. This was most likely the best place to catch the eels which were carried out of the sluice gate with the overflow water (ark is an old Scots word meaning the masonry in which the water wheel of a mill moves.) In 1508 the fishmarket appropriately moved to the edge of the Nor Loch. The Provost and his eight chaplains in the Trinity College Church were probably not best pleased with their new neighbour which was just on the other side of the dyke. Eventually the market moved back into the centre of the town. It was actually thought that the fishmarket and meatmarket were conducive to the spread of the plague because of the rubbish and mess they generated.

Eel pie was popular in the taverns of Edinburgh. Nor Loch trout, a well-known dish in eighteenth-century Edinburgh, however, did not in fact come from the Nor Loch at all. It was a stuffed haddock fried in bread

This view of Edinburgh c.1700 was drawn by Captain John Slezer. Calton Hill is in the foreground with three figures on its summit. Beyond it can be seen the Nor Loch with reed beds growing round its banks. The buildings on the edge of the loch housed tanning and leather working industries. A small island is visible at the far end of the loch.
(*By courtest of Edinburgh City Libraries.*)

crumbs and butter! The Scots dialect dictionary compiled by Alexander Warrack, 1911, in fact states that Nor Loch trout was a jocular term which was once used for a joint or leg of mutton. In February 1655, it is recorded that thousands of eels were thrown onto the banks of the loch as a result of stormy weather 'to the admiration of many'. Pigeons were shot on the banks of the Nor Loch as were wildfowl which were probably much more common in earlier centuries due to extensive areas of the country being bog and marsh.

The Nor Loch was a useful source of water for industry. As it was basically a static sheet of water little use could have been made of it for driving mill wheels. Most of these were found on the Water of Leith a short distance to the north of the loch at such places as the Dean Village and the aptly named Canonmills. Tan pits were located on the edge of the loch, where the Mound is situated today.

Cattle were driven into the town from outlying areas to be slaughtered within its walls, giving rise to an extensive industry in processing their hides and consequently tanning. In the Burgh records there are constant references to the concern expressed by the town officials about the waste and mess caused as a result of such activities being carried on in Edinburgh. In fact as early as 1556 a statute was passed instructing all the fleshers of the Burgh 'who slay sheep, swine and suchlike beasts to carry the filth of the same to the Nor Loch or out-with the Ports and bury the same under the earth'. Throughout the next hundred years there are similar references in the records. Originally the slaughterhouses were scattered throughout the town which compounded the problems of trying to keep the streets clean of waste products produced from these activities.

By 1642 certain fleshers had agreed to provide sufficient slaughterhouses outside the town or at the side of the Nor Loch. Many slaughterhouses, however, continued to operate throughout Edinburgh and in 1676 the Town Council proposed to remove all such activities to the banks of the Nor Loch. After a delay of several years, in 1681, the provost, in the name of the Town Council, instructed the Dean of Fleshers with all convenient diligence to go ahead with the plan to remove all the slaughter-houses in the Cowgate and other parts of the town to the Nor Loch. Land was purchased from Robert Hepburn who owned extensive tracts of ground surrounding the loch. The new slaughterhouses and fleshmarket were built on land on the east side of Old Provost's Close. It consisted of sheds and a tallow tron (market place) as well as a market for the landward fleshers. On 4 November it was reported that the beef market was almost complete along with the land fleshmarket. The fleshers in the mid-market were ordered to remove to the new fleshmarket by Martinmass and the landward fleshers above the Lucken Booths to the new fleshmarket below the beef market as soon as it was paved. On 7 December 1681 the new fleshmarket was opened and the licence for the old one withdrawn. This site today lies between Cockburn Street and the North Bridge.

There was also the problem of access to the new facilities as there was no direct passage to the banks of the Nor Loch from roads running into the Town. Cattle which arrived from areas to the north of Edinburgh had to be driven through the Old Port near the Canongate and then up the Royal Mile before finally going down a side street to reach their final destination. A new entrance was made in the town walls, appropriately known as the New Port, in conjunction with a new road through Trinity College Churchyard, just east of the dam for the Nor Loch. The new gate at the foot of Halkerston's Wynd enabled livestock to be driven directly to the slaughterhouses without having herded along the Royal Mile.

In 1716 the Committee of Public Works carried out further improvements to speed the passage of livestock through Edinburgh. The road from Bell-house Brae on Castlehill to Deacon Kincaid's Booth was enlarged and the Brae levelled so as to make it more passable in winter. The foot of the Brae was also fenced off so that cattle could not run directly into the Nor Loch.

Despite the provision of new slaughterhouses on the edge of the Nor Loch, in 1683 the Town Council complained that fleshers were still killing livestock in the old ones and taking their meat to the old fleshmarket. Cattle at this time were also being driven through the streets to be slaughtered on the south side of the town, to the danger of children and in spite of protests by the inhabitants. The Town Council revived their former acts with the penalties for failing to obey, and enacted that any flesh brought at the old land fleshmarket would be forfeited and the animals killed elsewhere confiscated.

Skinners dressed the hides of the slaughtered animals and made them into gloves and purses. This activity was concentrated on the banks of the Nor Loch but owing to congestion following a large increase in this profession, a number of the businesses moved to the Water of Leith in the seventeenth century. Leather was usually treated by soaking it in open pits flooded with water. There were two distinct classes in the manufacture of leather in Scotland from the thirteenth century onwards: the shoemakers or souters, and the skinners or glovers. The former confined themselves to the tanning of hides and the making of leather into boots and shoes, while the latter made gloves, purses and other articles from the lighter and smaller skins which they dressed. Flemish weavers were at this time found throughout Scotland. Several of them made their home in Edinburgh and were provided with houses, workshops, money and material for manufacture. Their skills were in great demand, hence the willingness of the town to provide them with all the means of production. The Burgh records for 1601 state that ten pounds was given to several cloth makers to pay for their houses at the Nor Loch.

There were in fact many buildings situated at the edge of the loch which was not without hazard to their owners. In 1698 a tanner called

John Ferguson petitioned the Council that slaughterhouses and tanholes built on the south side of the Nor Loch had become flooded, and houses were uninhabitable due to the closing of the sluice gate in the dam. He appealed that the sluice be opened which the Council agreed to. The water level was then reduced by around ten to twelve inches (30cm).

This plan shows the head of the Nor Loch and the features associated with it. On top of them has been superimposed the more recent Victorian Street plan of Edinburgh. Note the slaughter houses shown on the south bank of the loch and Physick Gardens (Botanic Gardens) on its eastern margins. Close by is the medieval Trinity College Church and its hospital. The old route to Leith runs behind it with the more recent one indicated by the name 'New Port' at the head of the loch.

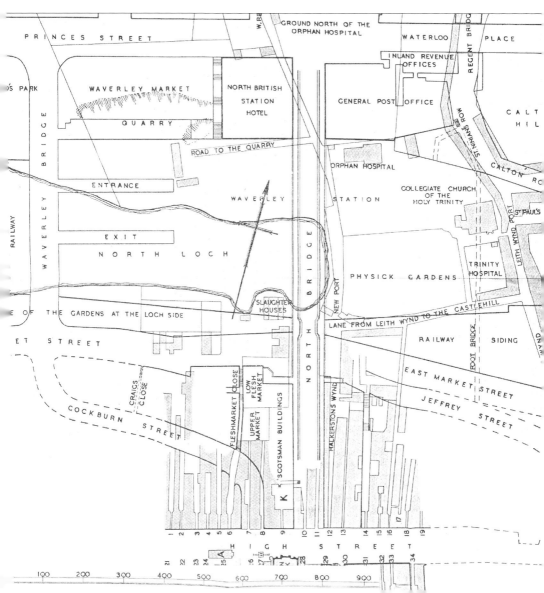

Not all industries were associated with livestock or the processing of their products. In 1684 the town granted a site on Castlehill above the Nor Loch for the location of furnaces for casting new bells as those belonging to Edinburgh's churches had become cracked and almost useless. The requirement for a large supply of water for the furnaces was probably why a site close to the loch was chosen; the area on Castlehill in fact became known as Bellhouse Brae.

Another activity carried on around the edge of the Nor Loch was that of quarrying. Up to 1425 most of Edinburgh's buildings were made of wood and straw and were prone to catch fire with disastrous consequences. From time to time there were devastating fires within the city which sometimes consumed large numbers of houses. When such catastrophes fell, the Nor Loch must have been used as a ready supply of water to douse the flames with the citizens scrambling down the banks to fill up their buckets. Laws were enacted which resulted in wood being replaced by stone for building. The largest quarries were on the north side of the Nor Loch and occupied a site where Waverley Market is today. They were known as Bearford's Quarries and stone was taken from them to build Trinity College Church which stood at the head of the loch. These quarries were worked for many centuries and eventually covered a large area. In the eighteenth century they were a source of stone for the North Bridge. By 1786 the workings were so extensive that concern was expressed that they would likely interfere with the construction of the New Town and particularly Princes Street. When the Scott Monument was built an old quarry of around 40 feet (12m) was discovered; consequently piles had to be driven far in the ground to support the monument.

The rock quarried from the north-east edge of the Nor Loch was a cream-coloured sandstone. Other quarries existed at the foot of the Castle rock which supplied stone to build the Wellhouse Tower and there were more near St Cuthbert's Church. In 1701 the Burgh Records relate that Robert Hepburn of Bearford was throwing 'the red [rubbish] of his quarry digged be him' upon the side of the loch as well as in it. In time it is said that his action would create a good and firm passage to Edinburgh. Despite this the Town Council decided to take action against his encroachment at head of the loch.

As long ago as the sixteenth century the citizens of Edinburgh had the right to dry their clothes on the banks of Castlehill just above the site of the Nor Loch. In 1768 a lease was given to Mr Trotter of a piece of ground at the side of the Nor Loch near Milne's Court (then in the process of being drained) for erecting an ice house to store ice cream. If the ice came from the Nor Loch when it was frozen, its cleanliness would certainly have been in doubt!

CHAPTER IX

Pollution in the Loch

WITH NUMEROUS INDUSTRIES on its southern banks, the Nor Loch became heavily polluted. It was also a relatively stagnant body of water which did not help matters. Many of the substances used by the skinners and tanners must have been unpleasant concoctions which would have ended up by being washed into the waters of the loch. In 1596 when gravediggers were digging a grave for Lady Jane Hamilton in the grounds of Trinity College Church, close to the head of the loch, evidence of the previous use of the site as a rubbish dump was uncovered. Bullocks' horns and an incredible quantity of sheeps' skulls were unearthed along with fragments of old Flemish quart bottles said to have been left there by the workmen building the church in 1460s. The Nor Loch also served as a 'free toom' (toom – a place into which rubbish is deposited) for refuse from the market aptly named the Shambles. In 1733 there was a clampdown on the use of the banks of the loch for middens, by which time some encroachments were stretching into the middle of the loch. Some of the dung deposited in the loch probably originated in the increasing number of carriage houses on the slopes of Castlehill immediately above the loch in the eighteenth century. A graphic description of the state of the loch is recorded by a group of skinners who described what it was like to work on its banks in 1684. As a place for washing skins and wool it had always been less desirable than running water 'so much more now when the fleshers reside at the side thereof, who by the running in of blood and excrements and washing of the tripes has so abused the water that all along the sides thereof with the heat of the sun it will be an ell deep of small vermine, so that by dipping the skin there it brings out ten times more filth than is put in with it!' (An ell is around 37 inches/one metre)

In 1731 the street leading east from the foot of Halkerston's Wynd along to the North Loch had become 'almost impassable by laying down great quantities of dung all along the foot of the brae which slips or washes

This picture entitled *View of Leith from James' Court, Edinburgh* by Clarkson Stanfield was painted in 1841 but depicts a scene from the closing years of the eighteenth century. The shrunken waters of the Nor Loch are visible at the bottom of the valley shortly before its final demise. Edinburgh is sprawling across the valley with buildings and huts encroaching on the banks of the loch. The North Bridge has replaced the earthen dam at the head of the Nor Loch as a means of communication across the valley. On the north bank stands a tall derrick-like structure, possibly a wind pump employed to drain the Nor Loch. (*Manchester City Galleries.*)

down into the street way and has quite ruined the calsey' (causeway). Presumably much of dung also ended up in the waters of the loch. The nuisance even affected Trinity Hospital next to Trinity College Church situated at the outflow from the North Loch. When the waters of the loch were high the building was cold and wet. When low, sewage and offal from the Shambles collected under the windows and beneath the floor, making the Hospital which housed elderly impoverished burgesses, 'noisome and unwholesome'. In 1704 the records for the Burgh of Edinburgh have an entry recommending that a dyke be built at the foot of Leith Wynd, on the east side opposite to Trinity Hospital, in order to clear that place of the present 'noysome puddel it is in' (harmful marsh). In the eighteenth century there was a drain that conducted sewage from Edinburgh Castle down the rock, discharging it near the Wellhouse Tower. An entry in the town records dating from 1740 mentions a disused quarry, close to this location, being used as a dump for snow cleared from the streets of Edinburgh. It states 'considering it is by permission of the

Governor and Deputy Governor of the Castle of Edinburgh that, for cleansing of the streets, the snow and ice which is carried off is laid in an old quarry on the north side of the Castlehill, when a thaw comes, and such snow and ice shall be melted and dissolved, to cause carry away whatever rubbish shall thence subside'. The waters of the melting snow presumably ran into the nearby Nor Loch along with horse manure and other animal droppings scooped up when the streets were being cleared. Although the Nor Loch was said to teem with eels and perch in the seventeenth century, both these species are often associated with heavily polluted reaches of waters as they can survive in conditions which would not sustain other fish.

The Burgh Loch was used to supply water to Edinburgh in the Middle Ages but the Nor Loch never seems to have been favoured for this role, other than perhaps for quenching the thirst of cattle being driven to market. The only exception to this was the water used to supply the Castle from the Wellhouse Tower at the edge of the loch. Springs located here also fed the Nor Loch. One of the earliest references to the loch in the burgh records dates from 14 February 1499/1500. The Town Council decreed that in times of the plague, or the pest as it was referred to in those days, all goods and houses in the town were to be cleansed using water and fire. It was stated that the cleansing by water was to be done in the running Water of Leith, 'and not in the South Loch or North Loch'.

Malaria (the 'ague') was rampant in Scotland in the Middle Ages. There were extensive areas of shallow water at the west end of the loch which would have provided ideal breeding grounds for the insect, although there is no documented evidence to prove this.

In fact one of the arguments for the draining of the Nor Loch was that it had almost been reduced to the state of an open sewer. A writer to the *Edinburgh Magazine* in 1790 says, 'The site of the Nor Loch is disgusting below as well as above the [north] bridge and the balustrades of the east side should be filled in as well as the west as they are only meant to show a beautiful stream and not a slaughterhouse.' Even when the loch had been drained leaving little more than a marsh in the valley floor, it still presented a health hazard. In 1816 Lord Cockburn penned the following uncomplimentary description of it: 'open on all sides the receptacle of many sewers and seemingly of all the worried cats, drowned dogs and blackguardism of the city. Its abominations make it so solitary that volunteers used to practise ball firing [target practice] across it.'

The River Tummel, which flowed out of the the Nor Loch, became more and more polluted. In the eighteenth century, this watercourse eventually took the outflow of three of Edinburgh's principal sewers. By the time the river had reached Restalrig it was referred to by the name 'the Foul Burn'. The cocktail of water and sewage was used to irrigate orchards and nurseries, on its journey to the sea, which ended at Craigentinny.

CHAPTER X

The Recreational Use of the Nor Loch

ALTHOUGH THE CONCEPT of amenity was unknown when the Nor Loch existed, it did have some value for recreational purposes similar to that of the open spaces of the Burgh Muir which was also in public ownership. This area was used to graze livestock, drill troops and provide firewood. Additionally it was used for golf and other sports.

The dookin of persons 'found guilty of anything that offended the Law

In this portrait of Douglas, 8th Duke of Hamilton, 1756–99, (by George Garrard) is depicted riding past the Nor Loch and Edinburgh Castle. The Duke had taken on a wager that he could ride from Edinburgh to Hamilton in three hours. He won.
   Some artistic licence concerning the Nor Loch and the Castle seems to have been employed by the painter! (*Lennoxlove House Ltd.*)

of God' from the pillar and stool by the lochside had provided a form of amusement as such occasions were always witnessed by large crowds who often hurled vocal abuse at the offender.

Archery seems to have been practised on the banks of the loch as in August 1592, Thomas Paterson, a merchant, was given permission to dig a well at the butts beside the Nor Loch. In those days archery would still be valued more for its military value than as a pastime. When Robert Hepburn, the landowner who often appears in references concerning land on the edge of the loch, sold some of his ground for the construction of a new slaughterhouse there were already preparations on the site for a tennis court and a bowling green. It is interesting to note that one of the first public bowling greens in Edinburgh was itself located on the former site of the loch in East Princes Street Gardens.

The houses belonging to the wealthier members of Edinburgh society had gardens which ran down to the edge of the Nor Loch. Many of them were laid out in a series of terraces descending the slope. These gardens were generally rectangular in shape and some had orchards while others grew vegetables. Where the loch waters lapped at the edge of gardens, often a boathouse was to be found. Boating was a popular form of recreation and in 1641 boat races were held on the Nor Loch but there is no record of this type of event being held again.

When the water of the loch froze over it provided great entertainment for the residents of Edinburgh. In 1632 there appears to have been a very severe winter as the Nor Loch was frozen from 29 November until 7 March the following year. Booths were erected on the ice, and all kinds of games were said to have been played on the frozen sheet of water including shinty and trap ball. A bonfire was even lit on the ice to roast a sheep. Prior to this there appears to have been another severe winter in 1606 when the frost lasted for over five weeks and games and competitions were held on the ice.

Other years when the Nor Loch was frozen over for long periods included 1653, 1670, 1692 and 1703. A writer commenting on the sliding and skating on the Nor Loch states that the frost seems to have been more severe in those days than now. Interestingly he was writing long before global warming had been acknowledged, his account dating from the closing years of the nineteenth century. To some extent his comment was true as Europe was in the grip of the Little Ice Age from the middle of the sixteenth century to the early eighteenth century, in fact for the greater part of the life of the Nor Loch. Its position would also exacerbate any period of frost by being on the north side of the Castle rock. Indeed for much of the winter the Nor Loch would remain untouched by the weak rays of the sun. Being in the gloom of the Castle rock or, further to the east, the shadows of the high tenements of Edinburgh, would mean that ice would persist at this location when it would have long since melted at neighbouring lochs which were in more exposed positions, such as the South Loch.

There was an old tradition in Edinburgh that it was unsafe to skate on the frozen Nor Loch after the beginning of February. Lord Fountainhall wrote: 'We have a proverb that the fox will not set foot on the ice after Candlemas (2nd Feb) especially in the heat of the sun and at any time the fox is so sagacious as to lay his ear on the ice to see if it be frozen to the bottom or if he hears the murmuring and current of the water.' Not all the inhabitants of Edinburgh were as cautious as the fox as there are several accounts of unfortunate persons falling through the ice and being drowned. In the diary of John Nicoll there is an entry for the year of 1661 which relates such an incident. He states that on 17 November, the day when Holy Communion of the Lord's Supper was being celebrated in all the churches of Edinburgh, two boys of reasonable age went down to the Nor Loch to play and pass their time upon the ice. The ice was not fully frozen and they fell through it and were drowned 'in miserable filth and dirt'. Rather callously John Nicoll ends this entry in his diary with the following comment: 'Let this be ane document to all prophaneris of the Saboth.' On 11 February 1682 three men were drowned when the ice broke.

Even when there was little left of the Nor Loch the remaining marsh still held an attraction to the young when it froze over. Robert Chambers, writing in the book *The Traditions of Edinburgh*, published in the nineteenth century, states: 'Yet many in common with myself must remember the by no means distant time when the remains of a few pools served as excellent sliding and skating ground in winter.'

Although ornamental parks for the public did not generally appear in Scotland until the middle of the nineteenth century, there is some indication that the Town Council had an appreciation of the loch as an aesthetic asset. The burgh records make several references to the fact that the Town Council placed swans and ducks on the Nor Loch. In 1591 the records state that a boll of oats should be purchased annually for feeding the birds during the winter. Edward Galbrayth was paid forty shillings for corn for the swans on the Nor Loch. In fact the earliest mention of swans on the Nor Loch occurs around 1584 when the tenant of the eel ark at the east end of the loch had also to feed the swans as one of the conditions of his lease. It is also recorded that the Masters of Trinity Hospital in December 1600 were required to provide a boll of oats for the swans for the coming winter.

Not all the citizens of Edinburgh had the welfare of the swans on the loch uppermost in their minds, as related in the following account: 'There were gay young men who found amusement in shooting at the wild birds of the Nor Loch from the windows of the houses overlooking it with hagbuts and others less responsible who tried their "dags" or pistols on the High Street and the wynds and forestairs adjoining, an amusement which once proved fatal to a woman passing by and very nearly as disastrous to the unlucky enthusiast of firearms who caused her death.' The death of the woman resulted in a proclamation forbidding the use of firearms in the streets and stairs of the Burgh in 1591. The killing of swans would not go unpunished either. In 1589 a man was accused of shooting a swan from his residence which overlooked the Nor Loch. This apparently was not an isolated incident. The accused was told to replace the swan he had killed and was forbidden to shoot at any bird on the Nor Loch from his house. This was a somewhat lighter punishment than that given to the trigger-happy marksman who killed the woman passer-by and narrowly escaped the death sentence.

In 1677 the Town Council was still concerned about the protection of the swans on the Nor Loch as they decreed that 'any person that kill or shoot or frighten or in any ways disturb the said swans under the pain of one hundred pounds attour such personal punishment be imprisonment and putting of the transgressors in the stocks as the magistrates shall think fit'.

At least one man was not deterred by this threat as in 1697 he was charged with the killing of a cygnet. His punishment was a large fine and, as in the case of a hundred years previously, he was told to provide a replacement bird. Up until 1700, however, shooting of wildfowl on the loch was allowed, though ducks and other birds were said to frequent the Burgh or South Loch in greater numbers than on the Nor Loch. Shooting on the Nor Loch of any creature was banned after 1700 as it was felt that indiscriminate use of firearms was posing a threat to the safety of the citizens of Edinburgh. Hunters had their activities further curtailed by the council which banned shooting beside the loch in 1730 because this 'makes the wild ducks and swans that are with expense and care brought and kept there for the pleasure of the inhabitants … fly away.'

In 1610 the Lord Provost, John Arnot of Plewlands, presented four black swans and four white swans to the town. The reference to black swans must refer to black-necked swans which originate from South America. It

This map of Edinburgh by William Edgar was printed in 1765 and is an updated edition of a work first produced in 1742. The Nor Loch or North Loch as it is worded on most early plans is shown as 'now drained' on the 1765 map but was very much in existance when the original one was printed. A year later in 1743 the sluice was opened and the water let out of the loch. The dimensions of the area covered by the loch on Edgar's map are 1,700ft in length (520m) and 400ft in breadth (120m). This excludes the area to the west of where the Mound now stands which is shown as a marsh on the 1742 map. Also note the large quarry on the north bank of the loch. Numerous gardens occupy the southern banks.
(*By courtesy of Edinburgh City Libraries.*)

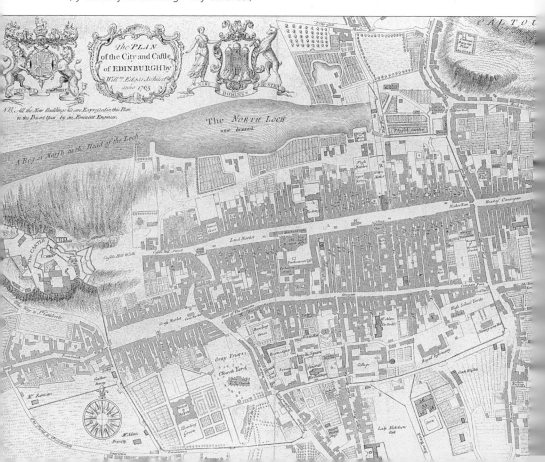

is highly unlikely they were completely black swans as they come only from Australia which had not been discovered in the early seventeenth century. This was not the first gift of these birds to the town as around 1590 Baillie Drummond gifted four swans to be put on the Nor Loch to make a flock of swans 'which will be very pleasant to be seen swim in the loch'. However there was a two-way traffic with the swans as in 1697 the Council granted Sir James Dick of Prestonfield permission to take two swans from the loch on condition that he replaced them at a later date. He wished to establish a flock of swans on Duddingston Loch which was adjacent to Prestonfield House.

The swans appear to have been well looked after by the Town Council as not only were they provided with food in the winter, but also with a hut for shelter. It was located at the front of a close which possibly was responsible for giving Swan's Close its name. In 1690 the hut became a subject of a dispute between the owner of the ground on which it was situated and the Council who owned it. George Wilson and his wife Rachael Crawford requested that the Council grant them a yearly rent of twenty pounds for all the bygone years and the same amount for future years. If their request was not met they threatened to remove the shelter. Twenty pounds in those days was a substantial sum particularly for the rent of what was a birdhouse! A compromise was agreed by which the Council agreed to pay six Scots pounds in back rent since the time the shelter was built and six pounds for every year in the future.

Mention must be made of the numerous other species of birds, now long since vanished, that would have frequented the banks of the Nor Loch in the Middle Ages. Red kites and ravens lived on the Castle rock and scavenged in the streets of Edinburgh. In the fields opposite the Castle rock could be heard the ceaseless calls of the corncrakes. All have long since vanished from the centre of Edinburgh. Occasionally pedestrians walking along Princes Street can catch a glimpse of swans overflying the city on their way to Duddingston Loch or further afield. It is not unknown for young swans that have become too exhausted to fly any further land on the site of the former Loch at Princes Street Gardens. They have to be rescued by the park officers and eventually transported to more suitable surroundings.

In the late nineteenth century it is recorded that woodcock, snipe and duck were to be seen near the ruins of the Wellhouse Tower, attracted by the dampness of the soil there which was once under the waters of the Nor Loch. Ducks breed most years in Princes Street Gardens despite the fact that the only water found there now is the Ross Fountain.

In 1968 there was a feature in the local newspaper about a duck which nested every year in St Cuthbert's Churchyard neighbouring the Gardens. It stated that it was probably the same duck that had been nesting at this site for the previous seven years. The article said it was most likely due to inherited instinct which went back to the days of the Nor Loch.

Military conflict gave rise to another pastime in the valley of the Nor Loch, albeit very temporarily. In the siege of 1573 mentioned earlier on, nearly 3,000 'great shot' were fired against the Castle. The bullets for the most part were recovered with the besiegers paying the local inhabitants a 'baubie' for every bullet returned to them. The banks of the Nor Loch must have swarmed with prospective 'treasure hunters' looking for ordnance that had fallen short of its target. Even when the age of sieges had long passed into history the valley of the Nor Loch still resounded to the sound of gunfire. During the Napoleonic War in the early years of the nineteenth century the 'volunteers', a form of Home Guard, used the site for target practice. Even though the loch was partially drained, the soldiers had great difficulty in crossing the valley floor to examine their targets as it was said to resemble a swamp, which could only be negotiated in very dry weather and then only at one or two locations.

Finally there were several popular walks round the loch. One of them used a route down Castlehill and along the foot of the Castle rock by the Wellhouse Tower. In the early eighteenth century there was a footpath that ran along the northern edge of the Nor Loch sandwiched between the water and a dyke which demarcated the limit of Hepburn's land. This route was called the 'green walk' because the path was covered in grass. At the end of the seventeenth century and in the early eighteenth century the routes of some of these walks became blocked by landowners encroaching on the banks of the Nor Loch.

Today one of the biggest crowd-drawing events in Europe takes place in the Princes Street Gardens situated on the former bed of the Nor Loch, namely the fireworks display which marks the end of the International Festival. Firework displays do not seem to be new to the location, and it is recorded in the diary of Sir John Lauder in an entry for June 1688 that

The valley of the Nor Loch c.1775 after the water had been drained. The North Bridge is visible in the distance and the Castle rock is on the right. Today the valley is occupied by Princes Street Gardens. (*By courtesy of Edinburgh City Libraries.*)

there were celebrations to commemorate the birth of a son to King James VII: 'At night there were curious fireworks at Nor Loch side.'

In the early years of the twenty-first century an artificial outdoor skating rink has been created in the weeks before Christmas as one of the 'Winter Wonderland' attractions for festive visitors. Appropriately this sheet of artificial ice lies in the East Princes Street Gardens on what was once the bed of the Nor Loch. After a gap of around three centuries the shrieks and laughter of people enjoying the pleasures of hurtling over a frozen expanse of water resounded in the valley once again.

CHAPTER XI

The Landscape Around the Nor Loch

URING THE EXISTENCE of the loch, the landscape around it remained relatively unchanged. The Nor Loch was in part responsible for this, acting as a brake on any advance of the town of Edinburgh in a northward direction.

The Castle overshadowed the western end of the loch although it must be remembered that in the Middle Ages this fortification would not have had the same dominance over the area. The walls that now extend to every corner of the rock were generally confined to the eastern end of it during the Middle Ages. By the late seventeenth century, the fortification had lost its medieval towers and had begun to resemble the present day structure. It may not, however, have presented such a stern appearance as around this time as the Duke of Albany is recorded as having purchased huge amounts of whitewash for it. Some or all of the Castle may have been painted white. It would certainly have presented a picturesque site standing on a high rock with the waters of the Nor Loch lapping at its base. Further down the hill, the houses and tenements of the town which were at this time among the tallest in Europe loomed over the widest part of the loch. Between the houses and the water were gardens on the relatively steep slope of the ridge to which the town clung. The gardens were rectangular in shape and around 150 yards (137 metres) long. Many of the highest ranks in society lived in Anchor Close and its immediate vicinity only a few hundred yards from the loch. At that time the neighbourhood was beautifully adorned with shrubberies and trees laid out in the terraced gardens which terminated at the loch's edge. From this location, there were uninterrupted views of the country beyond, as far as the Lomond Hills in Fife. In between some of the gardens were buildings which housed various industries such as bell making and textiles. There was even a dairy farm in this area.

In the days before the Industrial Revolution it was not unusual for farms and industries to be found side by side. There was also a small cluster of houses and buildings on the very edge of the loch, approximately where the Mound is today.

The influence of religion around the Nor Loch was particularly strong, with churches at either end of the body of water. Near the western end stood St Cuthbert's Church (or West Kirk), which in the seventeenth century was said to resemble a barn but became increasingly elaborate as it was rebuilt to repair damage sustained by various sieges. The choice of site for this church is somewhat enigmatic. It nestles in a hollow close to the former course of a tributary of River Tummel. A Christian cell is said to have been founded here by St Cuthbert, making it one of the oldest sites of Christian worship in Scotland. Many early churches were in fact established on pagan temples or sacred groves. Perhaps St Cuthbert's Church stands on a pre-Christian place of worship which could have been connected with the river or marshland in the Nor Loch valley. An early route from the Castle to South Queensferry and the north passed close to the early church. This place of worship, however, stood in a lonely spot particularly at night; except for one farm steading 'there was neither hoose nor ha' nor fire nor candlelight' between it and the villages which stood on the banks of the water of Leith. In 1597 a stone wall

Edinburgh and the Nor Loch viewed from the Lang Dykes, the road that ran along its northern side. This view dates from around 1720. (*By courtesy of Edinburgh City Libraries.*)

was built round the church to keep grazing horses and sheep out. The church was rebuilt numerous times over the centuries. In the sixteenth century it had only a thatched roof and it certainly was not a robust building. Rather than renovating the church it was decided in 1593 to erect a second church, known as the 'Little Kirk' which stood until the middle of the seventeenth century. On Sunday 27 September 1772, the imminent collapse of the church was feared. Tradesmen gave their verdict that it was beyond repair and should be replaced. The following year work on the new church commenced and it opened in 1775. In 1789 a steeple was added to the tower. Although the church was completely rebuilt again in the late nineteenth century these two features were retained and survive into the twenty-first century. The land around St Cuthbert's Church and within a short distance of the western edge of the Nor Loch has been used as a place of burial for around a thousand years. When the foundations were being dug for the new church in 1773 the workmen made a macabre but fascinating find. A leaden coffin was discovered which contained some bones and a leaden urn. Upon opening the urn, a most fragrant smell issued out. They found a human heart finely embalmed and in a good state of preservation. No inscription was on the coffin. It was thought that the heart belonged to a crusader killed in the Holy Land. It was the custom to send the embalmed heart home to the crusader's family. The burial ground in the sixteenth century was on a 'knowe' [knoll] south of the church. In 1789 marshland on the edge of the site of the Nor Loch was drained to provide further land for interring the dead.

At the other end of the Nor Loch, a short distance beyond the dam stood Trinity College Church. This was far more recent than St Cuthbert's Church which had its origins in the Dark Ages, dating only from the late fifteenth century. It, however, occupied the site of a former chapel of St Ninian which may have been a place where Christian worship had been practised from an early date. Trinity College Church was founded in 1460 by Marie of Gueldres in memory of her husband James II. It was erected in the hollow below the south-west shoulder of Calton Hill. Although it was a far more lavish structure than its counterpart at the opposite end of the loch, it was never finished. It did, however, serve as a parish church in the sixteenth century. When excavations of the Trinity College Church took place in 1848, shortly before the structure was

The western end of the Nor Loch in the eighteenth century. St Cuthbert's Church is situated in the centre of the picture. On the left side is the Castle rock and at its foot the Wellhouse Tower. (*By courtesy of Edinburgh City Libraries.*)

dismantled, it was discovered that the floor had been repeatedly raised until the bases of its pillars had become covered in from attempts to counteract the increasing dampness.

St Giles Church, situated further away from the loch than the other two, towered over the eastern end due to the fact that it was on top of a ridge while the other two churches were in the valley floor. It was appropriate that persons 'fund guiltie of anything that offends the Law of God' were dooked within the shadow of the crown-shaped spire of this church.

It is thought that the population of Edinburgh in the sixteenth century was between 9,000 to 15,000 people and was the largest town in Scotland. In total contrast to the densely packed urban area on its southern shore the entire area on the north side was almost completely devoid of any structure or house. The only exception to this was a hamlet on Multree's Hill, a little to the north of the dam for the loch. Dingwall Castle was also situated here although its life came to an end in the seventeenth century, long before that of the Nor Loch. The building was quadrangular with a tower at each corner. The large open tracts of land on the north bank of the loch remained totally untouched until 1763 when the North Bridge was built and the construction of the New Town commenced.

Prior to that the area appears to have been used for growing crops. In 1689 there is a record of besiegers of Edinburgh Castle being discovered in cornfields very near to it on the north side. Early maps of the area also show extensive areas on the north bank of the loch given over to crops. From 1128 to 1538 the monks of Holyrood Abbey owned the ground on which Princes Street now stands but in those days it formed the northern banks of the Nor Loch. In 1538 Abbot Cairncross of Holyrood, one of the greatest churchmen of his time, transferred these lands to his brother. James Hepburn of Bearford gained control over the ground in 1645, and it passed in and out of his family's ownership until it was acquired by the town in 1716.

Although the Nor Loch was an obstacle to communications, there was a footpath on the earthen dam that served as a route between the north and south side of the valley, acting as a short cut between the High Street and settlement known as Multree's Hill. The main road from the north entered the town at Leith Wynd where the eastern end of Waverley Station is today, then it skirted round the dam and the grounds of Trinity College Church next to it. Another roadway, known as the Long Gait or the Lang Dykes because of the walls that bordered it on either side, ran parallel to the loch following a route approximately taken by Rose Street today. The Lang Gait features in the history of at least two famous historical characters, one of whom was Mary Queen of Scots. On a September morning in 1561, the Queen rode along this road escorted by French knights and a large number of Scottish nobles; the party then made its way round the head of the Nor Loch and proceeded up to the Castle where they dined. In 1689 Claverhouse, with his party of dragoons, traversed the Lang Gait when heading for the Highlands where he intended to raise an army for the deposed King James VII (James II of England).

One description of the area stated that the sides of the loch, as well as its upper and lower ends, were fringed with trees and shrubs similar to the thick woodland near the Castle rock. This however is somewhat at odds with the evidence of early prints and maps which show a landscape bare of trees except perhaps for a few orchards near the town and some clumps of trees around the side of the loch close to where the Mound stands today. In a landscape that was almost devoid of woodland there were probably relatively more trees around the loch than elsewhere, although it would be by no means dense woodland.

This picture shows Trinity College Church c.1780 which stood close to the head of the Nor Loch, on a site now occupied by Waverley Station. Behind the Church is Calton Hill on whose summit is the Old Observatory. This Collegiate Church was founded in 1460 by Marie of Gueldres in memory of her husband James II and was dedicated to the Holy Trinity, The Blessed Virgin, St Ninian and All Saints. It occupied the site of a former Chapel of St Ninian and was next to the main road to Leith. It is perhaps in connection with the earlier religious site that influenced the locating of the church on poorly drained ground a short distance below the dam that formed the Nor Loch. When excavating in St Ninian's Row, close to the site in 1815 a quantity of fine red samian ware was found, perhaps evidence that this location may have had some form of spiritual significance even in pre-Christian times.

Trinity College Church according to one source was one of Scotland's finest mediaeval buildings. The structure, however, was never fully completed. The building was used as a Parish Church from 1580 to 1848. Part of the church was rebuilt in Chalmers Close off the High Street and can be visited today. (*By courtesy of Edinburgh City Libraries.*)

The Nor Loch was the subject of several sketches and paintings in the seventeenth and eighteenth centuries. In fact the first sketches of Edinburgh were made by the English invaders of 1544 but give little insight to the nature of the loch then. Many of the pictures which do depict the Nor Loch give a somewhat misleading impression as they all portray it in an idealised form full of water. Maps and plans from the latter part of the seventeenth century and eighteenth century record the area underneath the Castle rock being a marsh or bog. The paintings made around the same time are at odds with this evidence, showing the water extending almost to the edge of St Cuthbert's Church at the western end of the valley.

On some occasions the water level probably did extend this far but only in exceptional cases after perhaps the sluice gate was repaired and there had been heavy rain. Flooding of the valley would have happened fairly regularly in those days as the water table was believed to be at a much higher level than that of today.

On its south bank, the town wall skirted the edge of the loch, starting at Wellhouse Tower at the foot of the Castle rock then altering course to run up Castlehill where it reached the site of the Mound. One possible explanation for this is that the town wall was not considered necessary where the loch was deepest. Thus where the wall ran next to the Nor Loch it was relatively shallow and the sheet of water was not considered sufficient means of defence alone. There could be another explanation for the lack of a town wall east of where The Mound is today, with the evidence coming from an entry in the burgh records for 1569. Concern was expressed in regard to the residents of the town who lived close to the Nor Loch who were demolishing the closes without permission to make yards and open spaces. The town authorities said such actions were compromising the security of Edinburgh. It is possible that the town wall was not thought essential where the buildings were closely packed at the edge of the loch, forming an artificial barrier due to their dense nature. Their demolition, however, would reduce the effectiveness of this form of 'barrier'.

The western part of the loch became increasingly shallow throughout its history as it silted up and became full of refuse. In several places there were places where it could be crossed on foot and thus would have been little deterrent to a besieging army.

CHAPTER XII

Land Disputes Around the Nor Loch

Throughout the seventeenth and eighteenth centuries there was an increasing number of disputes concerning landowners encroaching on the edge of the loch, which was public property. As Edinburgh tried to burst out of the confines of the medieval walls, the pressure on the land round the loch increased as local property owners eyed up this under-used asset.

The problem did not end once the Nor Loch was drained. There were several lengthy legal battles in the nineteenth century concerning the rights of land ownership and most of them centred on determining the actual extent of the valley covered by the water of the loch and hence the area owned by the City. With the opening or closing of the sluice gate at the dam the land immersed by water could vary greatly in size over a very short period of time. In 1859 there was a case which involved the principal officers of Her Majesty's Ordnance versus the Lord Provost, Magistrates and the Council of the City. The dispute involved 'Whether the esplanade of the Castle of Edinburgh, the banks on each side of it and the ground round the base of the Castle rock belong to the Crown or the City of Edinburgh'. The second point of contention was that if these parcels of land belonged to the Crown, where was the boundary line between the foot of the north bank of the Castlehill and the ground known as the Nor Loch, which belonged to the City? Was it the line of the old stone dyke marked on Sibbald's plan of 1805 as the old boundary dyke between the town and the Crown lands, or was it a line further south, identical or nearly identical with the old town wall (which was on the edge of the Nor Loch)? A great deal of evidence was produced on the historical aspects of the Nor Loch but perhaps the most astute comment was made by Lord Deas who said the dispute would have been a lot easier to solve if the Nor Loch had been a natural loch (because it would have had a well-defined margin as a result of a constant water level) and not an artificial one. The judge was actually quoting an Edinburgh historian Maitland who witnessed the disappearance of the water in the loch when the sluice was opened in 1743.

In fact one of the earliest recorded disputes concerning the Nor Loch centred on the water level. In December 1600 John Dalzell was in dispute with the Town Council whom he accused of inholding water resulting in the flooding of his lands at the west end of the Nor Loch. The waters were let out of the loch so that Dalzell's land might be examined. John Dalzell's complaint eventually reached the Lords of Session with King James VI in attendance. In 1601 the dispute was settled when the Town Council agreed to pay John Dalzell the sum of £225 compensation. In contemporary records he describes himself as a 'heritable feuar of all and sundrie the Kirklands and gleib of the parroche Kirk of St Cuthbert under the Castle wall'. Kirklands lay to the east side of St Cuthbert's Churchyard in what is now West Princes Street Gardens. It is also interesting to note that the explanation put forward for the rise of water that flooded John Dalzell's land was the construction of a wall at the opposite end of the loch.

The ground of Kirklands had its boundary marked where it met that of the Nor Loch by march stones. Many years later in 1661, certain councillors were appointed to visit the march stones at the head of the Nor Loch and also check to see if any stones were missing and required replacing. March stones continued to be used as a means of defining the extent of the land owned by the Council in the valley of the Nor Loch until the mid-nineteenth century. Some of those placed in Princes Street Gardens in 1862 to mark the boundaries of land owned by the City and that owned by the Crown can be seen today.

Exactly a hundred years after the 1601 case there was another dispute regarding the level of water in the loch. Lord Fountainhall gives an interesting account of the incident in his writings. In 1701 Robert Malloch brought a case against the Town Council for closing off Halkerston's Wynd Port which was the entrance into Edinburgh for the footpath across the top of the dam. In the hamlet of Multree's Hill, which lay at the opposite end of the barrier on the north bank of the loch, resided a number of weavers and tradesmen. They operated in open defiance of the incorporations of Edinburgh whose authority did not extend outside the town walls. The tradesmen and their organisations felt threatened by this free enterprise zone only a stone's throw from their premises. Some of them put pressure on members of the Town Council to curtail the activities of the freebooters in Multree's Hill. The magistrates bowed to their pressure as elections were in the offering and they did not want to upset influential friends and supporters; they reacted to this commercial threat with the closure of the gate at Halkerston's Wynd which gave the residents of Multree's Hill direct access to the town. Further to this, the sluice gate was shut to flood the small mound that was utilised as the footpath by the traders. Malloch raised an action in the Court of Session against the magistrates who eventually relented on their harassment of the free traders, possibly because they had exceeded their powers by the closing of the town gate and the flooding of the loch. The other factor for the council reversing their decision could have been that the elections had been satisfactorily concluded.

There is further evidence that the Nor Loch could be used as a political tool from an incident that occurred a few years earlier in 1698. John Ferguson, whom the Council admitted had been 'much damnified by the keeping up of the water in the Nor Loch', won his case against them. The water level was to be lowered and liberty given to him to fortify the house against flooding. This incident took place when there were numerous encroachments on the banks of the loch and it is suggested that the Council sometimes deliberately raised the level of the loch to flood out houses that were being built on the town's property. There was further trouble in 1702 when it was claimed the north shore of the loch belonged to the town as part of its defences and exception was taken to the owners of the property in the area who were incorporating this ground into their own fields.

In the Middle Ages very few fields were surrounded by walls or physical boundaries. In the seventeenth and eighteenth centuries farming methods were altering and the countryside was being divided up by stone walls or dykes. Thus some of the disputes could be attributed to the introduction of these changes in farming and not just the greed of landowners such as Robert Hepburn. Robert Malloch had put up a wall at the east end of the loch obstructing the Council in the riding of the town boundaries and closing the route of a pleasant walk at the side of the water. Robert

This picture depicts St Cuthbert's Church and the Nor Loch in the early years of the seventeenth century. The waters of the Nor Loch lap at the boundary wall of the church which comprises of a tower with several additions and a ramshackle collection of buildings clustered around its base. Throughout its history St Cuthbert's Church was rebuilt numerous times totally transforming its appearance on several occasions unlike other old churches which often retained a similar outward appearance over the centuries. (*By courtesy of Edinburgh City Libraries.*)

Hepburn was at the same time enclosing his lands of Lochbank at the west end of the loch. He had built no fewer than three walls across a route to St Cuthbert's Church. In 1703 Malloch disposed of the land between the track known as the Lang Gait and the Nor Loch to Hepburn. Three years later the Town Council once more protested against encroachment by the latter. In 1709 the Town Council appointed a committee whose task was to negotiate the purchase of 30 acres (12 hectares) of land on the north side of the loch, perhaps with the intention of reducing future conflicts over ownership. It is recorded in the Council Records that the dispute between the town and Robert Hepburn went beyond heated discussion. The Town Treasurer on behalf of the magistrate and Council of the Burgh made a visit to the encroachments of this landowner. His wall was said to have impeded a walk on the north side of the loch called the 'good town's green walk'. The Town Treasurer snatched a spade out of one of the workmen's hands and then proceeded to throw some of the earth out of their cart. Legal documents were then placed in the hands of a Robert Seaton, a notary public.

However nothing came of the attempts to solve the dispute over land ownership at the west end of the loch for several more years. It was eventually settled when the Council granted Hepburn the feu of the mire and he would in return renounce all his claim to the marshes of the loch. The agreement, which was made in 1711, allowed Hepburn to water his livestock on the north side of the loch. The Council, however, did not forget the welfare of the swans either as they reserved the right to feed the birds upon Hepburn's side of the loch. In 1716 the town finally purchased the land of Lochbank from Robert Hepburn with the intention of developing it. It was another fifty years, however, before Princes Street and the New Town took shape on this ground.

As the town property came under threat the Council openly showed their concern in upholding their interests by the custom of the Riding of the Marshes in 1701. When the representatives of the town rode around the town boundaries they recorded in the Council Minutes that they had encountered several encroachments.

The next Riding of the Marshes was in 1718. This time they found 'many encroachments by local lairds and prominent Edinburgh Merchants' which had been complained of at the previous Riding of the Marshes but it would seem that a lenient eye had overlooked these transgressions in the intervening years. After the Riding in April 1718, it was agreed that the committee on public works should Ride the Marshes once a year and the whole council once every seven years.

CHAPTER XIII

The Reclamation of the Nor Loch

A S THE LOCH was artificial, the sluice gate needed constant attention if the water level was not to fall. Throughout its life the Nor Loch seemed to go through cycles when the water level was kept fully topped up and then eventually allowed to decline sometimes to the point of exposing the bed of the loch. Once this happened it usually spurred the Town Council into taking action to restore the water level to its original height. The burgh records refer to repairs made to the sluice gate on several occasions, although rather surprisingly there is little mention of the dam, presumably made of earth, used to hold the water in.

On 6 July 1554 the Town Treasurer was ordered to make a sluice at the east end of the loch for holding in 'the water thereof'. Shortly after the end of the siege of Edinburgh Castle, which lasted from 1572–73, on 25 November 1573 a further reference is made to the Nor Loch when an instruction was given to dam and hold in the water. There is mention made of four men being paid to repair the dyke at the east end of the loch in 1553–54. Another item in the Town Treasurer's accounts for the same year refers to work done on the 'Land Stank' (drain) on the side of the loch, beside Mr John Thorton's yard. Possibly the 'Land Stank' was the name given to the outlet channel at the head of the loch. The town records for July 1568, express the concern of the baillies and council that the Nor Loch was dry and could be crossed by man and horse at its western end. To remedy this twenty-three workmen with shovels and spades were employed to dig ditches at the head of the loch. Each of them was to be paid one shilling a day. Edward Henderson, master of works was appointed to oversee this work. The following year the sum of £54, was confiscated from William Smith and his wife Black Meg, hanged for concealing the plague, and was given to Adam Fullertoun, a baillie, to spend on a wall at the edge of the Nor Loch and the well at the foot of the Castle rock.

There is further reference in the following year to the council's concern for the defence of the town. James Nicolson, a writer, had surprised them by carrying out building work in his garden on the edge of the loch. They did not wish to have 'the auld common passages' reserved for the defence of the town destroyed by this development.

Further references are made in the Burgh accounts in the next century to maintenance work associated with the upkeep of the loch. In 1677 'The dovecot in the yard of Trinity Hospital to be demolished at the expense of Mr. Sutherland who has likewise undertaken to lay with flagstones the ditch that conveys the water from the North Loch through the yard and to line it with stones and lime on both sides of said ditch.' In 1702 an effort was made to reduce the amount of smuggled goods being brought into the city. The burgh records mention that a committee was appointed by the Council and suggested the following improvement to the sluice gate to increase the water level of the loch: 'a double tree eighteen foot long [5.5m], be fixed about the middle of the dyke where the sluice is, the one end fixed in the said wall or dyke and the other end supported by a jeast or stake fastened in the loch and that the same maybe fenced by close spar between the said stakes and wall'.

Although there are references until the middle of the eighteenth century to efforts to restore the water level to its ancient limits, the will to preserve the loch had begun to wane among the members of the Town Council. In 1716 the town purchased the lands of Lochbank on the western edge of the loch from Hepburn. During November 1720 a minute to the Lord Provost makes the following unsympathetic reference to the loch: 'The good Town being now possessed of the estate of Lochbank and the Nor Loch being rather a nuisance than a convenience to the City'. Another indication of the indifference to the loch was shown during the Jacobite Rebellion of 1745: when Bonnie Prince Charlie's army was approaching Edinburgh, no attempt was made to close the sluice gate and raise the water level of the loch. The concern about smuggling also seems to have diminished by the mid-eighteenth century.

Although no direct attempt to drain the valley floor had yet been executed, the historian W. Maitland stated that the soil of the town was constantly running into the loch, which was about half filled up in 1753 and that probably in less than a century it would be completely filled in. It must be also pointed out that even natural lochs have a limited lifespan as the streams that flow into them deposit sediment where the two waters meet. As most of the springs were at the west end of the Nor Loch, this area would have been particularly prone to nature's work of land reclamation. The Council does seem to have acted to maintain the boundaries of the loch which belonged to the Town, despite the ever-increasing number of encroachments on its margins. There must have been persons within the Council who possibly thought that the demise of the loch would be an opportunity for a land grab. Perhaps such persons turned a blind eye to the upkeep of the loch and the sluice gate, awaiting their opportunity to encroach on its margins.

The Nor Loch was never very deep, one source stating that its overall average depth was about eight feet (2.5m) but in many places was no more than three or four feet deep (1m), thus making it particularly susceptible to silting up caused by man-made or natural influences. As early as 1568 it was recorded that the Nor Loch was dry and passable at the west end by man and horse. As the centuries progressed the area of marsh at the head of the loch increased while the extent of the actual loch diminished.

Quarrying operations on the margins of the loch also resulted in waste material being dumped at the edge of it contributing to the infilling of the valley. Rather ironically the open space of land which was used for the construction of Edinburgh's New Town, leading to the final demise of the Nor Loch, owed its existence to this sheet of water. When the town burst out of the medieval city walls which had restricted its development for many centuries, its expansion to the north was blocked by the Nor Loch. Hamlets and castles could be found all over the southern margins of the town but there was hardly a single house on the north shore of the loch until the construction of the New Town. Although there was a loch on the southern edge of Edinburgh it did not represent the same obstacle to development, being situated on a relatively flat expanse of land, unlike the Nor Loch which was in a valley. During the middle of the eighteenth century it was recorded by Rev. Thomas Somerville that when standing at a window, looking out to the opposite side of the Nor Loch, then called Barefoot's (Bearford) Parks, there was not a single house to be seen. The Lord Provost George Drummond said to him, 'Look at those fields. You [Rev. Somerville] are a young man and may probably live to see all those fields covered with houses, forming a splendid and magnificent City. To the accomplishment of this, nothing more is necessary than the drainage of the Nor Loch and providing a proper access from the Old Town.'

Edgar's plan of Edinburgh produced in 1742 showed the area to the west of the present site of the Mound as being a bog or marsh. No doubt this marsh may have been occasionally flooded during periods of heavy rain restoring the loch to its previous size. There was also mention made by the Town Council of reviving the Nor Loch to its ancient limits after this date. On a later version of the same map produced in 1765 the Nor Loch is still shown as a fairly extensive sheet of water, but underneath its name the cartographer had added the words 'now drained', which was somewhat premature.

The first determined action to drain the valley took place in the early 1760s when the construction of the North Bridge was instigated. A Town Council Minute of 15 February 1764 states that the loch was 'now in a good measure drained'. Not all the water had, however, completely vanished as the Council decided it was necessary to expose the bottom of the loch in an effort to resolve some of the problems caused by the encroachments that had been taking place on the edges of the marsh. It should be mentioned that when disputes had arisen in the past about ownership of land on the margins of the loch it was deemed necessary to drain the water from the loch to expose the area involved before a settlement could be made. The Council also suggested that grass could be grown on the former loch bed which could then be cut by the citizens of the town, presumably to feed their livestock.

It is interesting to note that the North Bridge was built almost directly above the site of the dam of the Nor Loch. On the dam there was a pathway to the north. With the construction of the bridge the route was made very much easier, removing the descent through the Old Town to the shores of the loch. Part of the bridge collapsed during its construction due to the fact that the engineers had not taken into account the 'travelled earth' on the banks of the Nor Loch where large amounts of rubbish had been deposited since the Middle Ages.

There is further evidence that the valley remained in a marshy state after the early attempts to drain it. It is recorded in 1776 that the Town Council was in the process of digging a drain through the Nor Loch when a complaint was made by the artist Allan Ramsay, the son of the poet of the same name. The artist lived in a quaint house called Goose Pie, built by his father in 1740 on Castlehill, overlooking the Nor Loch. The nature of his grievance was that the drain came through the back of his property to its detriment. The dispute was the subject of a minor court case.

The most significant alteration to the valley of the Nor Loch in its history to date was the advent of the Mound. This feature cut directly across the valley in a north-south direction. Its construction commenced in 1783 and it divided the former site of the Nor Loch in two, although it should be pointed out that this structure was in probably many ways similar to the earthen dam that kept the waters of the loch in, but was on a very much grander scale. A clothier whose name was George Boyd is said to have been responsible for establishing a crossing place across the loch at this location. In spite of 'abominations', presumably a reference to the polluted state of the water in the valley, Boyd is said to have laid stepping stones across the marshy expanse to reach the north shore of the loch. Other citizens are then said to have followed his example until enough stones had been laid to form a causeway which came to be known as Geordie Boyd's Mud Brig. It also went by the less well-known name of 'Baillie Grieve's Brig'.

When the construction of the New Town was taking place it was decided to dump the earth excavated for the foundations of the new streets into the valley at the site of Geordie Boyd's Mud Brig with the intention of forming a direct route of communication with the Old Town. The effect of this huge mass of earth deposited in the valley would be to block the natural drainage channels running through the valley. By 1793 over one and a half million tons of earth had been deposited here. It was estimated that it took 1,300,000 cartloads to complete the Mound, a work 'unrivalled by any but Alexander the Great's at Tyre'. The nineteenth-century historian James Grant was less impressed with this monumental construc-tion: 'One of the greatest mistakes committed as a matter of taste was the erection of the earthen mound across the beautiful valley of the loch, from the end of Hanover Street to a point at the west end of Bank Street. It is simply an elongated hill, like a huge railway embankment, a clumsy, enormous and unremovable substitute for a bridge which should have been there, and its creation has been deplored by every topographical writer on Edinburgh.' In 1767 the Earl of Morton actually put forward a proposal for the construction of a wooden bridge between Warriston Close, near St Giles Cathedral, and the highest ground on the opposite bank of the valley. The magistrates however objected to the plan on the grounds that the property at the foot of Warriston Close was worth £20,000, a very large sum for that time.

Although one source states that the amount of surface water formed on the west side of the Mound was not very great, it does seem to have at least contributed to the survival of marshy ground on the site of what is now West Princes Street Gardens for another two decades. There is also a reference to part of the Mound subsiding by about 80 feet (25m) on the west side, while under construction. Perhaps this was attributable to the settlement of the dumped earth or maybe again to the compaction of extensive sediments deposited by long-extinct streams and lochs in the valley floor. It is possibly no coincidence that these alluvial deposits were found to extend downwards to a depth of 80 feet (25m) during surveys made in the twentieth century. There is a well-known painting depicting the Castle and the Nor Loch around 1780 by Alexander Nasmyth which shows the Mound under construction in the foreground. Rather surprisingly it depicts an extensive sheet of water on the west side of the earthworks as if the Nor Loch remained unaffected by the reclamation works in the final years of the eighteenth century. It is possible that this is due to artistic licence again. A half-drained valley bottom would not make the most appealing feature in a masterpiece. It is highly unlikely that in the twilight years of the life of the Nor Loch the waters ever lapped round the boundary walls of St Cuthbert's Churchyard for any length of time. There was a well-known route that ran to the east of the church and up to the banks of Lochside which would have been immersed under the loch had the waters extended this far. This exists today in the form of the busy footpath that runs through West Princes Street Gardens, from King's Stables Road, passing the Ross Fountain to exit at Princes Street opposite South Charlotte Street. Another painting dating from the late eighteenth century of the west end of the loch and St Cuthbert's Church also depicts an extensive sheet of water, even though it was supposed to have been partly drained by that date.

In 1787, the Town Council proposed that the drainage of the Nor Loch valley be completed as quickly as possible. Three years later in 1790, the

This sketch was drawn in 1816, shortly after the Nor Loch had been drained and the valley landscaped to create West Princes Street Gardens. The view is from the Mound looking towards St Cuthbert's Church with the newly built Princes Street on the right. On the left side is the Castle rock with the ruins of the Wellhouse Tower at its base. Note the wall extending along the left bank of the loch which originally formed part of Edinburgh's defences.
(*By courtesy of Edinburgh City Libraries.*)

Council approved a plan by James Gordon to dig a culvert the entire length of the loch bed from the North Bridge to St Cuthbert's Church. The first sewer constructed in 1767 only ran a short distance along the loch bed and is thought not to have extended any further west than the Mound. The new sewer would virtually reinstate the stream that ran through the area before the formation of the Nor Loch. It was intended to use this drainage channel to carry away the water from the Wellhouse Tower springs which in the past supplied water for the formation of the loch. A less pleasant role for this endeavour of civil engineering was that it was also to serve as a means of disposing of sewage. If all went to plan it was believed that the valley floor would become as dry as Princes Street itself. This ambition was, however, not to be realised for around another thirty years.

The condition of the valley floor in 1790 perhaps had acted as an incentive for instigating plans for its drainage as it was said in the *Edinburgh Magazine* to be in a disgusting state. Despite the attempts to improve the amenity of the site, little seems to have altered when in 1816 Lord

Cockburn wrote his well-known comment on the Nor Loch 'as being a receptacle of many sewers and drowned dogs', etc. Perhaps such a stinging description of an area so close to the recently constructed New Town drove the authorities to finally vanquish any lingering reminders of the Nor Loch. A statute was passed in the same year to drain the area west of the Mound. Mr Stevenson, a civil engineer, was asked to produce a plan to deal with the water coming through the common sewers in Princes Street, and that which came from the Grassmarket and Portsburgh.

In 1819 a contract for this work was given to John Ormiston, a mason who had a reputation for excellent workmanship. The work was to be completed before 1820 and at a cost of less than £2,000. Around the same time, when Princes Street Gardens were being laid out by James Skene, his record of the antiquities found in the loch bed describe them being covered in mud and there are also references to the workmen digging ditches. In about 1814 an old woman was found dead in a ditch on the former site of the Botanic Garden or Physick Garden as it was usually known, just east of the North Bridge. She had been hanging some clothes on a green there and had fallen into the ditch. She was unable to climb out and had been suffocated in the mud. This was evidence of the hazardous nature of the valley floor despite the disappearance of the loch. Not far from the site where this unfortunate woman met her end, the bones of three Celtic shorthorn cattle were found in 1870 when Waverley Station was being extended. They too may have blundered into the muddy banks of the loch that occupied the valley in prehistoric times and been drowned. More ominously the cattle could have been an offering to the water spirits.

In 1822 building work took place at Orchardfield, an area close to St Cuthbert's Church. The developers wished to drain the sewage from the new houses into the site of the Nor Loch. They stated that the right of the neighbourhood to do this remained unaffected by the improvements carried out by the Princes Street proprietors to the area. The Crown still had a vested interest in the springs that once fed the loch and as late as 1818 it was stated that 'the garrison [of Edinburgh Castle] should have free access at all times to the spring of water at the foot of the rock and to take and use the water there in'. There was a plan, proposed in 1803 but never executed, which intended to use the springs that flowed from the base of the rock near the Wellhouse Tower to supply the Castle with its needs for water. The principle was the same as that used by the medieval Wellhouse Tower but on a much grander scale. Two bomb-proof towers were to be constructed on the north face of the Castle rock, each housing a reservoir in its base. Unlike the medieval castle which received its supply of water by means of a simple hoist, each tower would be connected to the springs by a windlass and an endless chain of buckets to haul this much-needed commodity up the side of the cliff face.

One right that was not safeguarded, however, was the public's access to the former site of the loch. For many centuries they had been able to walk round its shores or use its waters for all manner of recreational activity.

Once the drained valley floor west of the Mound had been transformed into gardens only a privileged few had access to the grounds, namely the owners of the houses in the New Town. The initial idea was to create an area of woodland, perhaps not unlike the landscape that existed in the vicinity in prehistoric times, before most of the trees were felled. In 1820, five acres of the ground now occupied by West Princes Street Gardens were planted with a grand total of 77,000 trees and shrubs. The newly planted trees did not exactly flourish on the recently drained valley floor. A report written in March 1823 stated there were then about 8 acres (3 hectares) of ground on which stood over 34,000 trees plus a large number of shrubs. Out of this total only a meagre hundred or so trees remained alive a year after planting. This was attributed to the very slovenly manner in which they had been planted and the fact there were over 5,000 per acre (½ hectare). Dr Robert Graham, a Professor of Botany, was consulted to determine the number and the situation of replacement trees which were to be planted and to remain as permanent ornaments to the gardens. In the late 1860s West Princes Street Gardens fittingly reverted back to being in the ownership of the City and the grounds were open for all to enjoy. The area to the east of the Mound was also said to have remained in a marshy state until drained in 1821. Unlike the ground to the west, this part of the valley floor became a public nursery and then most appropriately Edinburgh's first public park in 1844. Fortunately the recreational value of the newly drained valley was realised at an early date and the Town Council took measures to protect the land from property developers. In 1822 there was a suggestion that the new Royal High School should be constructed on the bed of the now drained Nor Loch. Calton Hill was eventually selected as the most suitable site.

The shape of the valley which once cradled the waters of the loch has changed considerably since the first efforts were made to drain it. A book about walks in Edinburgh published in 1825 states that 'the principal place now appointed for the deposition of rubbish is that part of the Valley of the Nor Loch lying to the east of the Earthen Mound, which is to be filled up to a considerable height and afterwards laid out as pleasure grounds. There are upwards of a thousand cartloads deposited every day.' Thus the valley where East Princes Street Gardens is found today must have been considerably deeper in the days of the Nor Loch. In 1826 there was actually an objection made by the Princes Street proprietors about the infilling of the 'Nor Loch at the east of the Mound'. Their reasons for protest were that such actions were 'having the effect of injuring the romantic appearance of the Old Town as seen from this quarter', referring to the recently constructed New Town. They alleged that the Nor Loch valley had been filled up to the height of 24 feet (7.5m) with earth and rubbish. The Town Council did not deny this had happened but disagreed with the figure stating the real height was in fact only 16 feet (5m). It was suggested that if no more infilling took place and the area was covered in grass, the appearance of the site would not suffer from its increased elevation.

Even after the valley had been converted into West Princes Street Gardens the ghost of the Nor Loch returned on occasions to haunt its former home. Until 1854 West Princes Street Gardens suffered from flooding during periods of heavy rain and burst sewers. The Council was compelled to construct a great drain under the valley. Work commenced in 1854 under the direction of the well-known architect William Playfair. After the completion of this large sewer, the level of floodings diminished. Even today, however, during times of excessively wet weather, pools of water begin to form on the bottom footpath of West Princes Street Gardens. Occasionally photos of this flooding have appeared in the local press, often with captions such as 'The return of the Nor Loch'. It has not been unknown for the sewer covers to sometimes burst open and cover parts of the Gardens with a more potent form of liquid than water alone!

CHAPTER XIV

The Loch that Refused to Die

DESPITE THE NOR LOCH'S demise over two centuries ago, it still lives on in the minds of many of Edinburgh's citizens. Every so often plans to redevelop the city centre are featured in the local press, although most of the ideas put forward are never likely to leave the drawing board. Many of these schemes include some form of new Nor Loch in the vicinity of Princes Street Gardens. Around 1990 there was a competition for ideas to develop the site of Waverley Station. Several of these included gardens which featured pools of water being constructed over the unattractive station roof.

About the same time a small loch was created in the Gyle Business Park on the western edge of Edinburgh and the press referred to it rather inappropriately as the new Nor Loch.

Even when the Nor Loch existed it acted as an inspiration for the foundations of many grandiose schemes which like those of the recent centuries failed to progress beyond the drawing board. Most references to the Nor Loch mention a scheme by James Henderson as being the

earliest attempt to improve this sheet of water. The project is described in the burgh records of 1550–53, although it is believed to pre-date this, being first suggested in the reign of James V (1513–42). It was proposed to bring the Water of Leith into the Nor Loch and thus provide four fountains for the town. The scheme was described in the following terms: 'it being so much to the advantage to do so and of little expense, so that the town might flourish'. The fountains would supply water for drinking purposes. Nothing came of the project. Records in 1672 mention this plan again and the fact that no progress had been made since it was first suggested.

In 1593 an Italian merchant named Marques put forward a plan to link the Nor Loch with the sea. The shore of the loch was also to be deepened by one fathom (6 feet/2m). A report was prepared but no further action was taken. This, however, was not the last heard of this idea.

The Earl of Mar, who took part in the Jacobite Rebellion of 1715, was forced to flee overseas when it failed. His thoughts must have remained with Scotland as in 1728, while in exile, he proposed that a branch of the Water of Leith could be led into the Nor Loch from Coltbridge at Roseburn. The Earl's case for this proposal was stated thus: '… [it] would be to the great advantage of the convenience, beauty, cleanliness and healthiness of the town'. The scheme would have necessitated the construction of a ditch or drain just over one mile (1.6km) in length which would have probably followed a route similar to the Edinburgh-Glasgow Railway. The Water of Leith at Dean village actually flows within about half a mile (¾ km) of the former site of the loch, but at this location the river has dropped far below the level of the Nor Loch valley floor. Similar projects were resurrected over the next century but all to no avail.

George Drummond, the Lord Provost, who was the prime mover in the planning of the New Town, had little love for the Nor Loch but did not want to do away with it completely. His plan was to convert it into an ornamental canal. In 1776 it was recorded in print that the public 'will now be gratified with a pleasure-ground upon the south side of Princes Street to a considerable extent and the loch in time be formed into a canal which will not only be ornamental but of great benefit to the citizens.' Unfortunately the transformation of the Nor Loch into an ornamental canal was the only major part of James Craig's New Town that was never executed. The proposal, however, did get further than the earlier schemes, as some excavations for the channel itself were actually made at Waverley. According to the *Edinburgh Weekly Magazine* of 28 March 1776, twenty labourers 'began to work at the banks of the the intended canal between the Old and New Town'. How far their endeavour progressed is not recorded. A street in this vicinity was named Canal Street in anticipation of the completion of this work of civil engineering. The street survived for several decades before being demolished in 1868 when the station was extended. The canal is also actually shown on many plans of eighteenth-century Edinburgh as a feature that already existed.

Only a few years after the Nor Loch was completely drained, plans were being drawn up for its revival. The proponents of this idea stated that:

> ... the beauty of a lake reflecting the shadows of the romantic objects around would far excel any other mode of embellishment and there are ways of making it productive, skating tickets, pond fish, ice. The supply from the Wellhouse Tower has been calculated to be alone sufficient for the water but to secure a constant change of it, a pipe or covered drain from the canal basin which comes very near it would be at once obtained from the Committee and they would send it to you to get rid of the waste water which they say will be too abundant.

Like numerous other ideas nothing more was heard of it.

Although the above case for revival of the loch was primarily argued on grounds of amenity, another scheme which had origins dating back to the late sixteenth century was instigated in 1822. It envisaged the Union Canal which terminated at a point close to Lothian Road being extended through Princes Street Gardens to a point near Calton Hill.

A large inland harbour was to be constructed at the foot of the north slope of this hill, between Leith Walk and Easter Road. This was then to be connected to the sea via 'a grand canal navigable by ocean going vessels'. Plans were drawn up by engineers for the project and a map was engraved on a large scale. Those citizens of Edinburgh who were looking forward to watching cargo ships arriving from all over Europe in the centre of the city, were to be disappointed – the scheme got no further than the drawing board.

The advent of the railway put an end to any lingering ideas for the

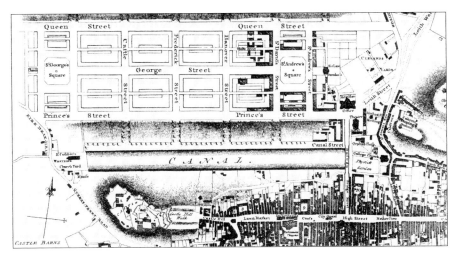

This plan of central Edinburgh dated 1778 depicts a canal on the site of the Nor Loch. Additionally at its eastern end there is a street named Canal Street. The canal was in fact never built but the street bearing this name was. It existed during the first half of the nineteenth century until it was demolished to make way for the expansion of Waverley Station. The canal depicted on the plan is actually a large ornamental pond and not intended for transport. Rectangular ponds were fashionable in the eighteenth century until they were superseded by those which mimicked natural-shaped bodies of water. There were, also, other plans which included a functional canal linking the centre of Edinburgh with Leith Harbour.

construction of canals through the centre of Edinburgh. To add insult to injury the railway was driven through the former Nor Loch valley, following a route very similar to that proposed for the canal. This was achieved despite extensive opposition to the railway running through the recently completed Princes Street Gardens.

Throughout the latter half of the nineteenth century the railway companies wanted to acquire more and more land from Princes Street Gardens. Their plan for expansion continued to be opposed by well-organised groups of Edinburgh citizens. They accused the railway of ruining the centre of Edinburgh particularly with the construction of Waverley Station. In 1890, when further schemes of expansion were in the pipeline, a brochure was published attacking the railway companies. The writer begins his onslaught with a poem condemning the way the valley of the Nor Loch has been developed:

Oh, ye apathetic citizens go to the centre of the Mound and behold there the valley of desolation, once made beautiful by the hand of God; now made hideous by the hand of man; then shall ye shun the folly of your fathers and curse the deeds of the destroyers; and your children's children shall praise your name.

The brochure also contained an illustration of how the Nor Loch valley could have looked if there was no railway line running through it. It shows the Nor Loch recreated and transformed into a great boating lake with landing stages for gondolas and boats plying its waters. Spanning the valley is a suspension bridge located close to the Scott Monument. The picture shown at the beginning of the chapter in fact resembles a scene not unlike that to be found on an Italian lake. The reality of having a loch on the north side of the Castle rock, which funnels winds along the valley and receives virtually no sunshine in mid-winter, would present a very different prospect from what is suggested in the picture and would not be quite so appealing.

It should be noted that the suspension bridge was not the first bridge to be proposed to span the water of the loch. The Earl of Mar, along with his plan to divert the Water of Leith into the Nor Loch in the first half of the eighteenth century, also suggested a bridge to be built across it. It was to span the head of the loch from the site of Liberton Wynd to St David's Street (if a similar bridge were built today it would run from a point close to Deacon Brodies pub in the High Street to St James shopping centre). King James VII also had plans for bridging the loch.

It is likely that proposals for the re-creation of a new loch in the centre of Edinburgh will continue to be made for a long time to come but like all the ones gone before, they will be no more than flights of fantasy.

In September 1988, the *Scotsman* published a letter entitled 'Bring back the Nor Loch'. Its suggestions, however, should not be taken too seriously.

Has anyone else considered the advantages of bringing back the North Loch of Edinburgh? The Festival could do with a boost and the attractions of the loch seem to be endless. Think of the added enhancement of water to the fireworks display. There could be fountains and waterfalls and an Aladdin's cave composed of Scotland's rocks and semi-precious stones. A tunnel underneath Princes Street Gardens could be built with some suitable see-through material, giving train passengers a glimpse of aquatic life as they arrive and leave Waverley.

Another equally implausable suggestion appeared in the *Evening News* in February 2004. Edinburgh based architectural firm, Sutherland Hussey, suggested a number of radical proposals for solving the city's transport problems. They included turning the centre of Edinburgh into an ultra-modern 'transport hub' with landing pads for vertical take-off and landing aircraft. It was also suggested that Princes Street Gardens be returned to a loch, acting as a runway for seaplanes! Close by there would be a central docking station for the seaplanes as well as for airships.

The firm's directors said the bizarre plans were intended to raise important questions about the city's future but they also believed some of their suggestions could one day become a reality!

CHAPTER XV

The Legacy of the Nor Loch Today

NEAR THIS SPOT FROM 1675 TO 1763
WAS THE EDINBURGH PHYSIC GARDEN,
ORIGINALLY FOUNDED AT HOLYROOD IN 1670
BY
SIR ROBERT SIBBALD AND SIR ANDREW BALFOUR, TWO OF
THE FOUNDERS OF THE ROYAL COLLEGE OF PHYSICIANS OF EDINBURGH.
THE GARDEN, UNDER THE CONTROL OF JAMES SUTHERLAND
THE FIRST REGIUS PROFESSOR OF BOTANY IN THE UNIVERSITY,
WAS THE DIRECT PREDECESSOR OF THE PRESENT
ROYAL BOTANIC GARDEN.

THIS PLAQUE WAS ERECTED IN 1978
BY
THE ROYAL COLLEGE OF PHYSICIANS OF EDINBURGH,
THE UNIVERSITY OF EDINBURGH AND THE
ROYAL BOTANIC GARDEN.

Opposite platform eleven in Waverley Station can be found a small plaque marking the site occupied by the Edinburgh Physick Garden between 1675 and 1763.

The garden sometimes referred to as the Botanic Garden, was overlooked on its western boundary by the earthen dam which formed the Nor Loch. Robert Sibbald was one of its founders and was responsible for acquiring the land for the establishment of the garden. He had studied medicine at Edinburgh University as well as in the Netherlands. It has been suggested that his experience overseas may have lead him to select a patch of low lying damp ground to establish his garden. Appropriately it had a pond for aquatic plants. The Town Council backed the enterprise which is mentioned in its minutes for 1677: 'This design will not only contribute to the good and ornament of the city but also prove exceedingly profitable for the instruction of youth in that must necessary the hitherto much neglected part of the natural history and knowledge wherein the health of all persons whither it be for food or medicin is so nearlie concerned'. By the late 1680s plants from Italy, Spain, France, Netherlands, the Levant and West Indies were growing in the garden and being irrigated by water running out of the head of the Nor Loch. By the mid-eighteenth century its role as a source for herbs for medicine had declined and it had become the favourite haunt of the literate and prosperous citizens of Edinburgh.

Ross Fountain, West Princes Street Gardens. The Ross Fountain is the only water feature in a valley once filled with water. It stands on the western edge of the site of the Nor Loch.

ALTHOUGH ALL VISIBLE TRACES of the Nor Loch disappeared when its drainage was completed in the early 1820s, some of the landmarks associated with its history survive. Perhaps the most notable is the ruinous Wellhouse Tower in West Princes Street Gardens. Today this is sandwiched between the foot of the Castle rock and the railway line. Its history is recorded in detail in Appendix X. St Cuthbert's Church still stands at the former margin of the loch. It is a useful reference point as this building features in many early pictures of the Nor Loch. The church bears little resemblance to that which witnessed the sieges in the sixteenth and seventeenth centuries. The structure that exists today is mainly a nineteenth-century creation and would dwarf the earlier places of worship on this site. The steeple is the oldest part of the building and was erected in the late eighteenth century. Within the church there is a room bearing the name 'The Nor Loch Room'. The North Bridge crosses the valley just west of where the earthen dam used to hold in the waters of the springs and streams. The most significant changes to the area itself has been the construction of the Mound which cuts the former site of the Nor Loch in two. Between the Mound and the North Bridge was the deepest and largest part of the loch. From the Mound to St Cuthbert's Church lay the shallower waters of the loch and its associated bogs and marshes. Little trace of the old town wall that ran along the edge of the loch from the Wellhouse Tower to a point close to the Mound survives. The name 'the Nor Loch' was used to describe the valley throughout much of the nineteenth century, long after the loch itself had disappeared.

The Lochs of Edinburgh: An Introduction

ALTHOUGH SCOTLAND is composed of some of the oldest rocks in the world, the landscape visible on their surface is in geological time very young. Until 15,000 years ago, the land was buried under an ice cap hundreds of feet thick. All the features of the Scottish landscape other than the hills and mountains themselves have been formed since the climate became warmer and the ice melted. The retreat of the glaciers resulted in huge amounts of water being released. This meltwater often ran across the barren landscape in the form of huge rivers which rapidly cut new channels to reach lower ground. Sometimes the meltwater became trapped behind remnants of the retreating ice creating large glacial lochs. Large areas of the Lothians were under water including Corstorphine and the area now occupied by Edinburgh airport. With the retreat of the glaciers the land began to be colonised by plants and animals. Elk and lemmings inhabited the margins of these early lochs. Many of these large lochs had a very limited life and disappeared once the water managed to break through the barriers that had restrained its flow or the ice had completely melted. The glaciers, however, had scoured out numerous hollows in the landscape and these often formed the basis of the lochs.

Some of these were formed on the site of the glacial lochs such as at Corstorphine. Other prehistoric lochs included the Burgh Loch at the Meadows, Gogar Loch, Holyrood Loch and Duddingston Loch. The latter loch is to only one to survive today. Like all physical features lochs and ponds have a limited lifespan. Hills and mountains often exist for millions of years but stagnant bodies of water may only be a feature in the landscape for a few thousand or even a few hundred years. Many of the hollows in which the lochs formed in and around Edinburgh were fairly shallow and soon became silted up. Sediments deposited by streams flowing into the western edge of Duddingston Loch from the Braids and Blackford Hill formed a flat delta there. Gradually the alluvial fans pushed back the water and spread over the greater part of the shallow basin, until eventually this part of the depression was completely silted up. The southern part of the basin whose total length at the end of the Ice Age apparently exceeded a mile, was probably shallow and the silting up was a comparatively rapid process, so that many centuries must have elapsed since the loch shrunk to its present area.

The same process was repeated at varying rates for the numerous other lochs and ponds scattered across the land now occupied by Edinburgh. By the time of the late Iron Age, the margins of the lochs formed in prehistoric times had probably already receded considerably. Many of the lochs and ponds, however, did not dry out completely but formed wide boggy marshes with reed-filled beds.

Although there were numerous hills in and around the site of Edinburgh, prehistoric man did develop settlements on the low-lying ground next to the lochs and marshes. A crannog (timber roundhouse built on an artificial platform of wood and stone in a loch or bog) is believed to have once existed on the southern bank of Duddingston Loch. During the late twentieth century evidence has been found of early settlements in the vicinity of Gogar Loch. The remains of an Iron Age fort were found at Redheughs, while construction work was being carried out at the business park at the Gyle. When it existed, it was probably protected by the waters or marshland of Gogar Loch immediately to the north. A Bronze Age field system which dated back 3,000–4,000 years was also found close by. This is evidence that even at a very early date not all the low-lying land in this vicinity was completely waterlogged or inhospitable. In medieval times a number of castles enhanced their defences by being situated close to the banks of lochs and marshes. They included Corstorphine Castle on the edge of the loch with the same name and Lochend Castle situated on a rocky outcrop. By the end of the Middle Ages, Edinburgh was still surrounded by extensive areas of bogs and marshes. The surviving lochs by this time, however, appear to have been in their twilight years. By the sixteenth century, the Burgh Loch which was Edinburgh's main source of drinking water appears to have been diminishing in size. A sluice controlled the flow of water out of the loch at the western end. Perhaps this was done in an effort to stem the diminishing supply of water provided by the loch.

The Nor Loch was actually a product of the Middle Ages, being created by building a dam and sluice across the valley. The site, however, had probably been occupied by a natural body of water when the glaciers melted. It probably dried out over the succeeding centuries along with several other lochs in the vicinity of Edinburgh. The move towards land improvement in the seventeenth and eighteenth centuries was the final death knell for several of the lochs that had managed to retain some vestige of existence. Their increasingly shallow and muddy waters were drained to form new fields and meadows for agriculture. The once extensive Gogar and Corstorphine Lochs succumbed to this fate as did the body of the water now displaced by the Meadows park.

Duddingston Loch by this time was only a fraction of the size it once had been in prehistoric times. In the early years of the nineteenth century it too was threatened with total oblivion as there was a plan to drain it completely to gain access to the springs of fresh water at the base of Arthur's Seat. It was then intended to use them to supply Edinburgh with drinking water. Fortunately this plan was never realised although the outlet for water from the loch was deepened resulting in it shrinking in size. Around this time the amenity value of the surviving lochs was beginning to be realised and this contributed towards their preservation. This, however, came too late to serve the small picturesque loch at Canonmills which was drained in the middle of the nineteenth century.

By the end of the twentieth century, the city of Edinburgh had expanded over the sites of most of the former lochs in the area. Unfortunately little research has been done on this subject by geologists and other disciplines since Victorian times. Most of the information on the origin and locations of the prehistoric lochs is based on papers written over a hundred years ago. There is also a lack of mention in contemporary records of any loch other than the Nor Loch situated close to the heart of Edinburgh. In the eighteenth century, during an upsurge in landscape painting, several artists recorded contemporary views of the Nor Loch for posterity. Unfortunately it appears no artist deemed Corstorphine and Gogar Lochs worthy of a picture. As with their history the appearance of these bodies of water along with several other lochs will remain obscure.

Besides the obvious landmarks such as Arthur's Seat, Blackford, Corstorphine and Calton hills, Edinburgh is built across undulating land with numerous hollows, ridges and minor slopes. In bygone centuries these lumps and bumps, which go unnoticed today, would have played a significant role in influencing the landscape. Most of the shallow hollows and depressions would have been filled with ponds or marshes, while the slightly higher ground next to them would have often been used for tracks and roads as well as settlements. Another difference from the landscape of today is that before the land was extensively drained the boundaries of the shallow lochs and ponds would not have been constant but would have varied enormously. In times of dry weather Corstorphine, Gogar and the Burgh Lochs may have almost completely dried out. After periods of continual rain they must have extended across the surrounding flat land to many times their normal size.

There are still one or two locations in Edinburgh where the state of the ground can be substantially influenced by the weather such as the Inch Park which was in prehistoric times on the edge of Duddingston Loch. For most of the year its surface is dry and can be easily walked across. After periods of prolonged rainfall great pools of water accumulate on its surface close to Inch House and much of the rest of the area becomes a quagmire. Murrayfield Stadium and the adjoining Roseburn Park has been flooded three times between 1985 and 2001. Not surprisingly this low-lying area was once under the waters of Corstorphine Loch. In 2003 Edinburgh's council estimated that 11,000 properties were at risk from flooding. Many of them were in the following areas: Roseburn, Stenhouse, Longstone, Duddingston and Peffermill, which were all once the sites of lochs and marshes. Finally, not only have many of Edinburgh's lochs disappeared in recent centuries but the streams and rivers that flowed into them have vanished. Many of the water courses still survive underground in sewers and drains, including the Tummel and its tributaries. Another stream that has disappeared from view is Broughton Burn. As late as 1850 it traversed the ancient village of the same name. A drawing made in the mid nineteenth century shows it spanned by small plank bridges and flowing through an area of huts resembling a western mining camp. Old maps revealed that its source was in the vicinity of Balfour Place, off Leith walk flowing to the head of the Kirkgate in Leith. Another stream that disappeared in the late nineteenth century had its source near Rossie Place close to the foot of Calton Hill. It then flowed north past Albert Street forming part of the boundary between Edinburgh and Leith.

In winter, low-lying mists sometimes can be seen hovering over the Meadows and expanses once filled with long-lost lochs. Perhaps they are the ghosts of these extinct bodies of water!

Surviving Prehistoric Lochs

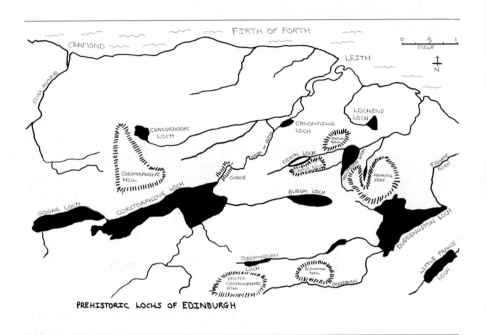

PREHISTORIC LOCHS OF EDINBURGH

Lochend Loch

THIS LOCH IS SITUATED less than a mile (2.5km) from the Old Town of Edinburgh and Arthur's Seat forms a prominent backdrop to it. It, however, is believed to have been only one of a chain of lochs that once occupied the south western portion of the low-lying ground that extends from Leith to the foot of Calton Hill. Until the recent past, there was a large pond of water on the Figgate Muir which is now part of Portobello. A little further to the north lay a fairly big sheet of water on what is now Craigentinny Golf Course. Over several generations this degenerated into a marsh which the golf course was constructed in the early twentieth century. There was also a deep pond on the north side of London Road

This picture shows Lochend Loch in the middle of the nineteenth century. It is depicted from its northern bank looking south towards Arthur's Seat which dominates the skyline. This landscape is probably typical of many of the lochs and ponds which once surrounded Edinburgh. In early prehistoric times there would have been dense woodland on the banks of such bodies of water, a feature almost totally absent in this picture. (*By courtesy of Edinburgh City Libraries.*)

which disappeared in the 1860s. Of all the lochs formed in prehistoric times, Lochend Loch seems to have undergone the least change. In the last few centuries it has shrunk somewhat in size but unlike Duddingston, which only covers about one tenth of its original area, the water of Lochend Loch has not retreated to anything like that extent. It has no streams of any size flowing into it and hence has not become silted up like the other lochs formed in prehistoric times. The main source of water is from springs which are clear and free of sediment. In the nineteenth century, the loch extended to within a few yards of Lochend Road and much of the grass area on its western side was also under water. In 1882 the dimensions of this sheet of water were recorded as 390 yards (356m) long and 160 yards wide (146m). By the end of the twentieth century the length has decreased to about 200 yards (182m).

On the eastern edge of the loch is a precipitous rock face, its appearance somewhat softened by the trees and shrubs that have colonised its slopes.

A formidable castle of which few traces remain once crowned the summit of this rocky outcrop. The building that now stands on the summit dates only from 1820 and incorporates some fragments of it. In the latter Middle Ages the Logan family owned the castle or Restalrig Tower as it was sometimes referred to. The fortification was in a strategic location guarding the eastern approach to Edinburgh, with Holyrood Palace being less than a mile away (2.5km). Situated on the only area of high ground in the vicinity of Restalrig and surrounded by a loch and extensive areas of marshy ground, the castle must have presented a daunting prospect to those intent on besieging it. A Norman adventurer, De Lestalric, built the first castle on the rocky knoll when King David I gave him a grant of land. This structure would probably have been built of wood but replaced in succeeding centuries by stone.

The English army under the command of Richard II managed to capture it in 1385 when Holyrood Abbey was burned. In 1560 the castle and village of Restalrig were again occupied by English troops, although this time they were allied to the Scottish Protestants. They were fighting French Roman Catholic troops who were besieged in Leith. By this time Restalrig Castle had taken on the appearance of a large house, according to a contemporary map. Just over a decade later when Sir William of Grange held Edinburgh Castle for Mary Queen of Scots, a battle was fought at Hawkhill, a rocky wooded knoll beside Lochend Loch. In a show of force, some of the garrison marched out of the Castle in battle order heading towards Leith. Regent Morton, who was in command of the opposing forces, engaged the superior forces of Sir William of Grange close to Lochend Loch. After bitter hand to hand fighting Morton put them to flight. As the routed army fled back towards Edinburgh and the safety of the Castle many of them were slaughtered in the narrow streets of the Canongate by Regent Morton's forces. At the end of the sixteenth century Lochend Castle was deliberately destroyed, not in any war but in a dispute about access. The structure lay close to an important track used by persons travelling between Leith and Edinburgh. Its owner, however, refused to allow public passage through his grounds and Provost Little of Edinburgh accordingly cast the building down with the tacit consent of King James VI.

Although most evidence of the castle has long since disappeared, another building from the same period survives virtually intact, namely the dovecote. When Leith suffered from visitations of the plague in 1645 it was realised that destroying the clothing of the infected person would create great economic hardship. Hence the sixteenth-century dovecote was converted into a fumigator and the garments of those struck down by the disease were transported to Lochend to be cleansed by heat and smoke. People who could afford to pay for the cleansing of their clothes were directed to another kiln, called Bessie Cooke's Kiln.

The loch was also used as a source of water for Leith in the late eighteenth century. The town was experiencing severe shortages of water as both its industries and population were growing rapidly. To alleviate this a wooden pipeline was constructed in 1754 to conduct the waters of the loch to a cistern in Leith. Critics of the scheme said that Lochend Loch was too small to meet the demand for water from Leith and that it was an unhygienic source anyway. Within a month of the pipeline being completed the critics were proved right. To increase the flow of water

Lochend Loch and the house of the Logans of Restalrig in 1847. The house incorporates the remains of Lochend Castle which once commanded the top of this rocky bluff. A hunter is depicted on the edge of the loch shooting waterfowl. Although this activity had been banned on the Nor Loch as far back as 1700, it continued well into the nineteenth century on other bodies of water close to Edinburgh including Lochend and Duddingston Lochs. (*By courtesy of Edinburgh City Libraries.*)

'the big pipes' were extended further into the loch to find deeper water. In 1793 despite this modification there was a drought and the water supply from Lochend Loch failed. Around 1800 house owners between Lochend and Leith had their properties connected to the pipe resulting in little water reaching Leith itself. It was not until the middle of the nineteenth century that Leith had an adequate water supply and this only occurred when water from other sources further afield was piped into the town.

Like the Nor Loch, this sheet of water had long been used for hunting and fishing. King James IV is recorded to have employed four boatmen to raise wildfowl here, and hunters were still shooting duck from the banks of the loch in the nineteenth century. In winter the frozen loch was a favourite with the skaters. Due to its sheltered position and calm waters, ice suitable for skating formed here before that on the nearby St Margaret's Loch. In the winter of 1890, the ice on Lochend Loch remained strong enough to bear the weight of skaters for no fewer than six weeks. The ice was eight inches thick. While the water was freezing the public were not allowed into the park, as the water here was deeper than at most other ponds. Playing by its banks was also discouraged, until the ice was strong enough to bear a person's weight. A rowing boat which resided in the nearby dovecote was run across the frozen stretch of water to test its strength before skating was allowed.

Local rumour said the loch was bottomless and some newspaper articles said the maximum depth was around 120 feet (36m). This appears to be a gross exaggeration as a map of 1817 denotes the deepest part being no greater than 22 feet (6.5m). Despite the fact that the margins of the loch had shrunk considerably since then, the depth of the deepest part had remained relatively unchanged to the closing years of twentieth century. The ominous reputation of the loch was given substance when a horse and cart stumbled on its banks and fell in around 1922 or 1923. The creature was drowned and the cart never recovered. More unfortunate tragedies happened in 1958 and again in 1997 when schoolboys playing in its waters were drowned. There were calls after both incidents for the loch to be filled in but it has managed survive to the twenty-first century unlike so many other prehistoric lochs. In 1871 old timbers in the form of a large platform were exposed by the shrinking margins of Lochend Loch and at the time were claimed to be the remains of an ancient crannog. The wood was fast crumbling into mould when discovered but on careful examination it was determined that large logs had been laid on the ground at regular intervals. Some of them were of oak, but the greater number seemed to be of pine with the bark in many instances still remaining. Between the logs was found a mass of rich black mould, intermixed with nuts and fragments of small branches. The remains of the wooden structure extended along the shore of the loch for a distance of 120 yards (98 metres). This crannog, however, is more likely to have been a timber trackway, often termed a corduroy road, and may have been only a few hundred years old. Today the loch, which in reality is now a large pond, is the centrepiece of a public park, surrounded by houses. The placid nature of its waters give little hint of the many dark events associated with this location.

Duddingston Loch

DUDDINGSTON LOCH is the largest surviving natural loch in Edinburgh. Now only a fraction of what it once was in size. The loch was originally about a mile (1.6km) in length and breadth. It extended as far south as Cameron Toll Shopping Centre and the Inch Park. The waters of the loch may have lapped round the site of what is now the Inch House, as access to the castle which stood on this site was by means of a drawbridge. Inch in fact is an old Celtic word for island. Closer to Duddingston Loch is an area know as Bawsinch which like the Inch is on the 150 foot contour line (46m) and it may have been surrounded by water. Braidburn and the Pow Burn drained into the western part of the loch causing it to be filled in with silt from this end. Another smaller loch once existed close to the western end of Duddingston Loch when it extended to the Inch. It was situated on the east side of Liberton road and centred on the junction of Gilmerton Road. It probably was part of Duddingston Loch before the water level dropped. During periods of heavy rain the waters of Duddingston Loch may have reached as far as the eastern end of Blackford Hill. In medieval times much of the area to the south of Peffermill Road was still marshland and was a refuge for bandits and robbers until the seventeenth century. The area to the east of Duddingston Loch was also an inhospital area as evidenced by the fact that William Wallace and 200 of his followers found shelter in the Figgate Whins, prior to the successful raid made by him in 1297 on the north of England. In Victorian times,

Duddingston Loch, Edinburgh. This loch is the largest body of water inside the city boundaries.

the trunks of large oak trees were found in abundance in the old peat moss at Cameron Toll close to Duddingston Loch, as well as embedded in the clay of the Figgate Burn at Portobello. At Portobello, there was at one time a considerable estuary, which in the process of time came to be silted up with drift sand from the beach, leaving only a narrow channel for the Figgate Burn.

The area occupied by Duddingston Loch today would have been the deepest part of the prehistoric loch, situated in a glacial hollow gouged out during the last Ice Age. The main source of water for the loch are springs flowing out of the foot of Hangman's Rock and Girnal Craig. The dimensions of the loch today are around 1,740 feet in length (530m) and 790 feet in width (240m). The area of water is about one tenth the size of what it was when Duddingston Loch was formed in prehistoric times.

Evidence of Mesolithic and Neolithic flints and stone tools indicate man has been living around the margins of the loch since as early as the 5th millennium BC. The most spectacular find was made in the waters of the loch in 1778 when marl was being dug from it. Over fifty items including spearheads, swords and the handle of a feasting bucket were recovered. The objects dated from the late Bronze Age (1000–750 BC) and may have been an offering or sacrifice to the gods or water spirits which the owners of the items believed to dwell in these waters. More ominously, human remains including skulls were recovered at the same time. Some of the objects were gifted to King George III and Sir Walter Scott. Today many of these Bronze Age treasures are in the care of the Royal Museum of Scotland. There were several hill forts and prehistoric settlements on the slopes of Arthur's Seat, perhaps due to the fact that most of the low-lying ground was marsh or under water. In the early nineteenth century a collection of timber piles or staffs set at irregular intervals could be seen firmly bedded into the bottom of the loch. They were located not far from the southern edge of this body of water and may have been the site of a crannog.

Duddingston village, situated on the north-eastern banks of the loch at the foot of Arthur's Seat, is of great antiquity. Its origins are thought to date back to the seventh century when it was known as Treverlen. King David gifted the land to the Abbot of Kelso at the beginning of the twelfth century. The Abbot in turn leased the land to a Norman knight called Dodin. The knight named the village West Dodynstane which

eventually became Duddingston. A trackway followed a route above
Duddingston Loch from the village to Edinburgh. Unfortunately the
settlement stood on the route of invading English armies intent on
plundering Scotland's capital city. The thatched cottages of Duddingston
suffered frequently in the ensuing years of warfare during the reigns of
Edward II and Richard II. In such times of strife, the inhabitants are likely
to have taken refuge among the beds of reeds that surrounded the loch
and marshes. During the sixteenth century Scotland was again suffering
from invasions from the south. In 1547, at the Battle of Pinkie, near
Musselburgh, the Scots army was defeated by the English under the
command of the Duke of Somerset. Many of the fleeing Scottish soldiers
headed towards the safety of Edinburgh but were slain by the enemy
before they could reach the protection of its walls. Some of those who
managed to escape would have passed through Duddingston and the
Windy Gowl, a narrow pass above Duddingston Loch.

Further bloodshed occurred when Kirkcaldy of Grange was holding
Edinburgh Castle for Mary Queen of Scots. He was on the Burgh Muir
waiting to escort vital supplies into the besieged town when the Regent's
forces descended on him through the Windy Gowl. A few months later
the situation was reversed when they chased the Regent's troops back
through the Windy Gowl and into Duddingston where they gave battle.
The Windy Gowl today is marked by a road cutting through a rock face
a short distance before it reaches Duddingston, and lies close to the edge
of Duddingston Loch.

In 1745 Prince Charles' Jacobite Army camped on the gentler slopes
around the loch before and after the Battle of Prestonpans. Their
commander stayed in Duddingston village and was not exposed to the
same hardships as his soldiers.

Civil strife was also witnessed on the margins of Duddingston Loch,
one such incident commemorated by the name Murder Acre on its western
banks. In 1677 it was the scene of a riot by youths employed in various
trades who were informed by the city magistrates that they could not
take part in a parade to celebrate the birthday of Charles II. Between
1,500 to 2,000 people gathered there to demonstrate at the imprisonment
of several persons who had clashed with the town guard in protest at the
ban. Soldiers from the King's Troop were ordered to break up this
gathering of protesters. Despite having instructions to fire above the heads

of the crowd, several trades youths and their supporters were mortally wounded when the troops charged the crowd.

A couple of decades earlier Duddingston Village suffered from an outbreak of the plague and many of the 140 persons who perished were buried on the northern banks of the loch.

In the last few centuries military and civil conflicts fortunately have been relatively infrequent interruptions to village life in Duddingston. It was an agricultural settlement where weavers also made a living by gathering the reeds that grew on the fringes of the nearby loch. They then stripped the reeds and wove them into a coarse fabric known as 'Duddingston hardings' which was then sold in Edinburgh. The same plants also supplied a source of thatch for the local cottages. It was renowned for its strength and the hardness of the fibres which withstood the attacks of sparrows, mice and common vermin. In 1670, Sir Robert Murray, the new owner of the loch, informed the residents of Duddingston that they could no longer use the loch for fishing, laying of lint or washing but they were still permitted to water their horses and cattle.

A century later there were about 5 acres (2 hectares) of reeds at the western end of Duddingston Loch but few grew at the opposite end as this was where the cattle and livestock were allowed to drink. In the late nineteenth century the trefoil plant was gathered from the loch in the month of June for local medical laboratories. During the first half of the nineteenth century increasing demands were being placed on Duddingston Loch as a source of water for a variety of uses. In 1807 a lease provided for a tenant to take water from Duddingston Loch to supplement that in the Figgate Burn dam for use by nearby mills. It was agreed with the proprietor of Prestonfield who owned the loch, that the level of it should be reduced by two feet (½ metre), thereby draining some of the surrounding land. It was also proposed that all leases granted to tenants should contain a clause making them bound to reduce the level of Duddingston Loch.

In 1824 there was a plan to use the loch as a new source of water for Edinburgh. The scheme involved draining the water, which was about 9 ft deep (2.7m), and connecting up the natural springs by pipeline to the capital. It was intended to install a stationary steam engine to pump the water to the required height. Fortunately it came to nothing as the intention was to drain the loch dry to expose the fresh water from the springs. There were, however, improvements made to the outlet of the loch which drains into the Braid Burn. The deepening of the water course contributed to a decrease in the size of the sheet of water, although it has retained a similar shape throughout the last few centuries. Two small islands, however, had appeared in the loch by the mid-nineteenth century due to the fall in the water level.

In 1795 the loch became the main centre for curling competitions for Edinburgh, when it replaced Canonmills Loch in this role. The octagonal tower, standing on the edge of the water near the church, was used by Duddingston Curling club. In 1803 this club prepared a set of rules for the game which have since became the standard regulations.

In the twenty-first century, the loch's main claim to fame has been as a wildlife reserve. Swans were first placed on its waters in the seventeenth century by the Duke of Lauderdale. When he died, his wife removed the swans to ponds by their country house. This enraged Sir James Dick, the owner of the loch, who demanded the return of the birds. When the Duchess of Lauderdale refused his requests, he broke into the grounds of her house, carried off the swans and placing them back on Duddingston Loch. This action led to a major legal dispute between the two. At the end of the eighteenth century, otters were recorded as living in the water here as were pike, perch and a profusion of eels.

The loch was also popular with skaters in the nineteenth century. The Edinburgh Skating Club, whose main venue was Duddingston Loch, claimed to have been founded in 1642. If this was correct it would be the oldest skating club in Britain. Its origins more probably date from the mid-eighteenth century as this sport is thought to have been unknown in Britain until 1662, when the first skaters were seen on the River Thames during the Great Frost. In the nineteenth century the skating club made use of Dunsapie Loch and St Margaret's Loch in addition to Duddingston. Vandals sometimes scattered reeds over the ice at Duddingston Loch, hampering the sport. In January 1837, the ice gave way and around a dozen persons had to be pulled from the freezing water. Throughout the nineteenth century the Skating Club looked into the possibility of improving on nature by developing an alternative venue. As early as 1828 it was suggested that it would be desirable to co-operate with the Curling Club in the search for a piece of ground in the neighbourhood of Edinburgh which could be overflowed with such a quantity of water as would freeze in the course of one or two nights sufficiently strongly to allow skating on it. It was thought it might be possible to find such ground 'in the vicinity of the Union Canal' but nothing more was heard of this idea. In 1841, the Club requested if a field below Fettes Row could be obtained, as it was considered that the ground could be easily flooded with water to a depth of two or three inches from a mill lead. However, no further action was taken. In 1881 plans were drawn up for a limited company to construct and manage a skating pond at Roseburn but again nothing materialised. The Edinburgh Skating Club continued to use Duddingston Loch throughout the nineteenth century with trips to other lochs and ponds around the city. The records of Edinburgh weather in the nineteenth century show it to have been variable. Many winters passed with no chance of skating or curling on Duddingston Loch. There was a period in the 1830s and 1840s when such activities were very infrequent here but in the second half of the century there was more ice even if only for a few days at a time. Nearly every winter there was skating for several weeks each season. The picturesque locality of Duddingston was also a favourite subject of both professional and amateur artists. Even the great artist J. W. Turner was said to have envied his friend, John Thomson, for his proximity to such an attractive sheet of water. The creation of a bird sanctuary at Duddingston in 1923 brought the activities of the Edinburgh Skating Club on this sheet of water to an end.

During its history Duddingston Loch must have claimed many lives. One of the more notable cases was that of the minister Mr Bennet from the nearby church whose body was found in the water a short distance from the manse in 1805. He was a naturalist of some ability and had recorded the zoology, geology and botany of his parish with the results of his labours being recorded in the entry for Duddingston Parish in the first edition of *The Statistical Account of Scotland.*

In the late nineteenth century the loch was already well known for its great variety of birdlife. Occasionally ospreys were recorded visiting here. Hunting was still practised at this time with wildfowlers shooting their quarry from rowing boats. In 1923 William Askew of Ladykirk presented Duddingston Loch and the surrounding land to the nation and two years later it was officially designated as a bird sanctuary. In 1971, Bawsinch on the south-eastern corner of the loch was purchased by the Scottish Wildlife

Trust. Artificial ponds were dug here and given the names Matthew, Mark, Luke and John. More recently a much larger pond was created and called Gunn Loch after a lifelong member of the Edinburgh Natural History Society.

Extinct Prehistoric Lochs

Canonmills Loch

SITUATED AT THE FOOT of the slope which the New Town now occupies land close to the Water of Leith, Canonmills Loch was little more than a large pond in the final centuries of its life. It occupied a natural hollow from what became the northern end of Dundas Street, extending eastwards to Rodney Street. Its northern limit was Eyre Place and Royal Crescent marks what was its southern edge. The close proximity to the Water of Leith perhaps extended the life of the loch with the floodwater from the river topping up that in the hollow. Its later role as a mill pond also perhaps prevented it from disappearing many centuries earlier.

When Canonmills Loch was formed in prehistoric times it may have been as large as Duddingston Loch is today, extending along what is now Henderson Row as far as Hamilton Place. In time numerous mills were built in the vicinity of the loch which gave rise to its name. During the late eighteenth century a mill lade (watercourse leading to mill) of considerable length siphoned water from the river at the Dean Village to serve its mills and those at Silvermills. The water then flowed eastwards into Canonmills Loch and returned to the Water of Leith by another lade which provided power for the water wheels of the mills.

The first mills were built during the reign of King David I in the twelfth century. A village grew up around the north and eastern fringes of the loch. One of the more interesting mills that existed at this locality was that devoted to the manufacture of playing cards. It was owned by Peter de Bruis or Brauss who also won the contract to install the scheme to supply piped water to Edinburgh from the springs at Comiston in the late seventeenth century. The loch was partially drained by the mid-eighteenth century leaving a small sheet of water at its north-eastern

This picturesque view depicts Canonmills Loch around 1830. A decade or so later the loch was drained. Note the fisherman on the bank of the loch and the partially submerged mill wheel on the far side. By the late nineteenth century this rural area had been engulfed by the northward expansion of Edinburgh. (*By courtesy of Edinburgh City Libraries.*)

end, close to what is now Broughton Road. Its dimensions were then about 300 feet (91m) in length and breadth. An alternative name for Canonmills Loch was Boyton Pond, the latter being now a more apt description for a body of water which by the end of the eighteenth century was only about four feet (1.2m) deep. Despite the limited amount of water in the loch, a brewery was constructed in the early nineteenth century which used it as a source of water. Canonmills House was built close to the loch by the owner of the lochside brewery.

As well as acting as a magnet for the economic activity in the area, the shallow body of water attracted fishermen who caught perch in what must have been increasingly polluted waters. Hunters also shot ducks and geese from its banks.

With the demise of the Nor Loch in the eighteenth century, Canonmills Loch took on its role in winter as being the main venue for curling competitions. Canonmills Curling Club claimed to be one of the oldest in Scotland and the sport was celebrated by an annual procession, including magistrates and councillors, who marched down the hill from Edinburgh to the loch. By 1847, the shrunken remains of Canonmills Loch could not fend off advancing urbanisation, and its waters were drained. The last portion was not completely drained until about 1860. The mill lades were put in drains or were diverted. In 1865 an artificial pool was created on the site of the former loch as part of the Royal Gymnasium. It was a cross between a theme park and a gigantic gym created with the intention of encouraging exercise among the youth of Edinburgh. The pool contained a large boat with room enough for 600 persons. It was known as the Great Sea Serpent. This apparatus took the form of a large roundabout set in a circular artificial pond, held fast by wire ropes attached to a central pivot. The circumference of the 'boat' was 471 feet (144 metres) and it was six feet wide (2 metres), equipped with 250 short oars. Those with the paddles would set the boat rotating in an undulating movement, assisted by eight paddlewheels which were turned by people on board the boat. It must have been an amazing sight and a memorable experience for the members of public on board. In building the Gymnasium, its founder John Cox faced a number of problems including a lack of water which was overcome when permission was granted to use a stream of water from a nearby railway tunnel.

The novelty of the Great Sea Serpent eventually wore off and it was replaced by ordinary boats. In winter a skating rink was formed at the Royal Gymnasium, 90 feet long (28m) and 75 feet broad (23m) using a thin sheet of frozen water which was illuminated at night by hundreds of lights. John Cox, was also responsible for creating Craiglockhart Pond.

Although the latter survives today, the pond at Canonmills which contained the Great Sea Serpent and other attractions had been filled in by the end of the nineteenth century. Only a small curling pond remained and that too eventually disappeared. The site of the small loch, with its interesting history, is now occupied by King George V Park and there is not a drop of water to be seen anywhere!

The Burgh Loch

ALSO SOMETIMES KNOWN as the South Loch or Borough Loch, it lay a short distance south of the medieval city walls and occupied an area almost exactly the same shape as the Meadows Park today. The sheet of water

The Burgh Loch or South Loch in the middle of the eighteenth century. By this time attempts had been made for nearly a hundred years to drain it and by then it must have diminished greatly in size. Many maps in fact show the site as being completely drained by the date this picture was painted! Stagnant pools of water, however, survived in the Meadows which were created on the bed of the Burgh Loch into the early nineteenth century. The large building in the painting is George Watson's Hospital, where the Old Royal Infirmary was later built. The viewpoint for this picture is probably from a point close to where Melville Drive and Marchmont Road meet today. (*By courtesy of Edinburgh City Libraries.*)

was about ¾ mile in length and about ¼ mile in breadth (1,200 m length, 400m wide). The area of water covered around 63 acres (25 hectares). The southern edge was marked by Melville Drive and on the north side by North Meadow Walk, next to the perimeter of the Old Royal Infirmary. Its western edge, which was the head of the loch, was at Brougham Street and the eastern limit, where the deepest water was, is thought to have been Hope Park Terrace. In a document called the Protocols of James Young, 1492, the area on the north east edge of the Burgh Loch is referred to by the name of Loch Flatt. In modern times this area lies between Lauriston Place on the west and Buccleuch Street to the east. An ancient lakelet existed near Bristo Port until early in the sixteenth century, its bed being discovered when digging for a drain in 1872. This small body of water may have been a relic of a once much larger loch centred on the Meadows due to its close proximity to it. Evidence for the Burgh Loch, which was formed in prehistoric times, was left in the form of peat beds and deposits of marl which were around three feet deep (0.9m). Bones of wild cattle, stag and elk were discovered in the nineteenth century when geologists excavated the former loch bed.

In the twelfth century King David I gifted the inhabitants of Edinburgh the land that bordered the Burgh Loch. It was used as common land for the grazing of livestock as well as for recreation purposes and was known as the Burgh Muir, from which the loch's name is derived. In the Middle Ages the Burgh Muir was covered with woodland which included many large oak trees. Some of these still survived around the waters of the loch in the early sixteenth century. Unfortunately not much is known about the historical events connected with the Burgh Loch before 1500 due to the destruction of many of Edinburgh's historical documents. The body of water must have been an obstruction to invading English armies intent on capturing the town.

The Burgh Muir was the mustering point for several Scottish armies preparing to invade England. In 1384, 30,000 men, some of whom were mounted on small horses, gathered here under the command of the Earls of Fife and Douglas. Many of their animals would have probably quenched their thirst with water from the loch before journeying south. A century later in 1482, James III led an army of 50,0000 men south from the Burgh Muir, a feat repeated by his son James IV in 1513 with disastrous results. His army was defeated at Flodden with great loss of life. Some of its soldiers would have drunk from the loch's water before journeying south, never to return. Blood must have been shed on the banks of the Burgh Loch on numerous occasions throughout Edinburgh's turbulent history. The warlike Edward III of England invaded Scotland in support of Edward Balliol with his claim to the throne in 1335. In August of that year a large body of foreign mercenaries from the Low Countries landed at Berwick-upon-Tweed and made their way north towards Edinburgh to campaign for the English king. The foreigners, most of whom were well armed and mounted on horses and under the command of the Count of Namur, were intercepted on the Burgh Muir, a short distance from Edinburgh. The Scots eventually put the enemy to flight but only after reinforcements arrived from the direction of the Pentlands. According to legend, when the armour was removed from the body of one of the foreign mercenaries

it turned out to be that of a woman! Many other of her companions fled
into Edinburgh but were promptly dispatched by the Scots. The remnants
of this once proud force found refuge in a then derelict Edinburgh Castle
but surrended the following day. In 1867, a great quantity of bones was
discovered about five feet below the surface where Glengyle Terrace now
stands. Contemporary sources state they were the casualties of this battle
although their origins probably have a more mundane explanation. Perhaps,
however, they mark the last stand of the foreign mercenaries trapped on
the banks of the Burgh Loch whose waters once lapped the edge of the
ground now occupied by Glengyle Terrace.

The Burgh Loch's surplus waters were carried off by the Dalry Burn
or Lochrin as it was often known. The latter name means the rin or run
of the loch and gives its name to an area at Tolcross through which its
waters flowed before eventually draining into the Water of Leith near
Roseburn. The Burgh Loch was the main source of water for Edinburgh,
other than the groundwells that were dug within the city walls. A dyke
and sluice existed from at least the mid-sixteenth century to control the
flow of the Lochrin out of what is now the site of the Meadows.

In many ways the Burgh Loch or the South Loch resembled its
counterpart the Nor Loch in that it had a dam and sluice at its head. In
the case of the Burgh Loch, this piece of engineering must have extended
its life and prevented its waters from disappearing at a much earlier date.
During the sixteenth century many regulations were issued for shutting
the sluice, as a consequence of the scarcity of water available for the
citizens of Edinburgh. On 25 May 1554, 'The baillies and counsale ordanis
the Burrow Loch to be biggit [built] up in sic manner as it salbe sufficient
to hald in the watter and quhat expensis salbe maid thairon salbe allowit.'
This action did not meet with universal approval as it reduced the amount
of water available for irrigation purposes from the Lochrin. John Lawson
of High Riggs took the law into his own hands by organising the destruction
of the dam so his own lands would be watered. A number of persons
were imprisoned for this act, although John Lawson's fate is not recorded.
This was just the first of several similar recorded attacks. In the years
1575 and 1582 water became so scarce that the brewers were prohibited
from using water from wells in Edinburgh. They were instructed to use
the water of the Burgh Loch for their industry instead. In 1598, the Town
Council proposed a scheme to bring water from the loch to four wells in

the High Street, but like so many similar ideas of its time it appears it came to nothing. Edinburgh was not only troubled by water shortages but by outbreaks of the plague. In 1520 and 1568 temporary shelters were built for the sufferers on the eastern edge of the loch, close to where Archers Hall in Buccleuch Street is today. Plague victims were, however, given strict instructions not to wash their clothes in the waters of the loch so that the drinking water did not become contaminated.

For a period of nearly twenty years control of the water of the Burgh Loch passed to the ale and beer brewers. The Burgh Muir had a long association with the brewing industry. In the early years of the sixteenth century William Dunbar, a Scottish poet, praised Edinburgh as a place for 'merriness' and for good living. Despite the apparent plenitude of fresh wines and fragrant clarets, the taste for beer prevailed among the inhabitants. An act passed in 1510 placed an obligation on all feuars of the Burgh Muir, on which the Burgh Loch was situated, to build kilns for the manufacture of beer. A public company formed under the auspices of the Town Council for the manufacture of beer and its operations extended over the Burgh Loch in 1597–98. The Society of Brewers however was forbidden to alter the run of the water of the loch, the surplus of which was to be made available to the inhabitants of Edinburgh. When their control ceased in 1618, due to problems with the payments of duty, the ownership of this resource returned to the Town Council. The water level had fallen considerably. By this time it was also becoming increasingly muddy and of poor quality, encouraging the search for alternative sources of drinking water and resulting in the construction of the pipeline from Comiston Springs nearly half a century later. During 1619 the magistrates are recorded again ordering the closure of the sluice to conserve water in the Burgh Loch but over the next few decades it continued to shrink. In 1649 the watering of horses was forbidden from the wells in the town and the stablers and owners of these animals were instructed to use the Burgh Loch instead. They were placing a great demand on the town wells with pumps that were, according to contemporary sources, easily broken. In 1657 the Town Council took the decision to drain what was left. A small body of water was to be retained at the east end of the loch for the watering of horses.

A failed attempt at reclamation in 1657 was reputedly carried out by 'English soldiers and finished by five poor Scotsmen'. During that year there was a bad drought and it was thought that if the loch was drained it might have alleviated the shortage of water in the wells of Edinburgh! 'At this tyme and by the space of many yeiris of befoir the town of Edinburgh was desitute of watter to serve thair housis and thair toun wellis wer dryed up so that the inhabitants could not be servite for want. The toun, taking this to thair consideration, they concludit to dry the south loche and to essay, gif the drying up of that loch might help this evil.' The English soldiers were given instructions to dig trenches to gather water in the loch bed. They began their work on 3 August 1657 and ended it before 20 September, having covered both sides of the loch except for a small area. The remainder was left to be finished by five needy Scotsmen. In 1658 John Straiton was given the lease of the loch which included the fishing rights. Perch and eels inhabited the muddy waters but were said to be of the kind not favoured on Scottish dining tables. John Adair's map of Midlothian, dated 1681, does not show a loch at this location, although the Nor Loch is still marked as a significant feature. It was in the seventeenth century that the name of the Meadows originated as cattle now grazed on the damp ground left by the receding water. Even in the preceding century the southern margins of the Burgh Loch dried out in summer and it was the practice of many poor women who owned cattle to cut the long grass that grew here to feed their animals. This activity met with the disapproval of the Town Council who in 1581 forbade them from gathering the grasses before midsummer's night, as it disturbed the birds that nested on the banks. This must have been one of the earliest laws ever passed to protect wildlife but its motive was probably to ensure hunters' interests were safeguarded.

William Carfrae and five others took over the lease from John Straiton and continued to tame the marshland. They laid out a walk on both the north and south banks as well as planting ash, fir and plane trees beside them. In 1722 the lease fell to Thomas Hope who continued the work of turning the muddy loch bottom into a landscaped park.

A windmill was erected near Buccleuch Street, possibly as early as 1598, to provide local brewers with a supply of water. It was intended to establish the necessary vats and other buildings for brewing on arable ground at Greyfriars Port. Water was to be pumped to the complex from the Burgh Loch in leaden pipes by means of one or more windmills. In the end, only one windmill was constructed. The water it pumped from the loch was stored in a large cistern which stood at its base. It measured 180 feet (55 metres) in circumference and survived to at least 1768 but the windmill had been demolished by then. Its memory is preserved in the name Windmill Street which skirts the north side of where it once stood, close to Edinburgh University. A second body of water also was to be found nearby. A row of buildings which stands next to Buccleuch Street bears a plaque with the name 'Guse Dub' – the Goose Pond. It was an established landmark before 1686 but was drained in 1715. This body of water was the subject of a satirical comment in Sir Walter Scott's novel titled *The Fortunes of Nigel* set in the reign of King James VI. One of its characters, Ritchie, was visiting London and became engaged in conversation with a Master George, '"I suppose you will tell me next you have at Edinburgh as fine a navigable river as the Thames with all its shipping?" stated Master George: "The Thames!" exclaimed Ritchie, in a tone of eneffable contempt, "God bless your Honour's judgement. We have at Edinburgh the Water of Leith and the Nor'Loch!" "And the Pun Burn, and the Quarry-holes and the Guse Dub, ye Fause Loun!" answered Master George sarcastically.' The Goose Pond was possibly evidence that the Meadows Loch once extended as far as the junction between West Crosscauseway and Buccleuch Street where it was located. It may have become an isolated body of water as the level of the loch retreated. A stream ran from the pond eastwards to St Patrick's Square. It then turned north down the hollow of Dummiedykes and joined the Tummel River at Abbeyhill.

Thomas Hope suffered great financial hardship while trying to improve the Meadows and died in 1771 before the work was complete. For someone involved in reclaiming land from water, he appropriately built a house in 1740 with a Dutch-style frontage on the banks of what had been the Burgh Loch. The structure survives today standing opposite the tennis courts in the Meadows.

There were still pools of stagnant water in 1806 and the site of the loch is said to have remained a morass until 1840. Lewis Spence, writing in the *Scottish Daily Express* in 1935, recalls that he had been informed by aged relatives that in the early years of the nineteenth century, ducks and water-fowl were still flushed out and shot on the banks of a fairly extensive sheet of water at the Meadows. The loch bed was still being used as a rubbish tip in 1871, with refuse piled to a height of 6 or 7 feet (2m), greatly altering the appearance of the former loch site. Rather surprisingly a plan for improvement of the Meadows Park submitted in 1855 suggested the creation of a large artificial pond on the western side. The Lochrin stream was still supplying water for cooling the condensation pipes at Haig's Distillery near Tolcross well into the nineteenth century. At the north east corner of the Meadows a small street still bears the name Borough Loch Lane. On one side of it is a group of old buildings which in the nineteenth century housed a brewery.

Corstorphine and Gogar Loch

LOOKING SOUTH TODAY from Corstorphine Hill, all that is visible in the foreground is mile after mile of roads and houses stretching towards the Pentland Hills. It is difficult to imagine that only around 400 years ago someone standing at the same viewpoint would have seen an extensive area of water at the base of Corstorphine Hill with ponds and marshland occupying most of the flat land beyond. Only a few buildings would be seen, with the main form of communication being a track taking advantage of the rising ground at the edge of Corstorphine Hill to avoid the marshy land.

Corstorphine Loch occupied the low-lying ground at the base of Corstorphine Hill and extended from Haymarket to Broomhouse, a distance of nearly three miles (5km). The head of the loch was at its eastern end where the loch was broadest being around ¾ of a mile (1.2km) wide. Its waters stretched from Corstorphine Road in the north to Gorgie Road in the south and covered much of Roseburn including the site now occupied by Murrayfield Rugby Stadium. It is interesting to note that during April 2000, Edinburgh experienced one of its most intense periods of rain for many decades and at one point the area occupied by the stadium reverted to being a 'loch' with 3 feet (0.9m) of water lapping over the pitch. The eastern end of Corstorphine Loch was the shallowest part and the first to be filled in by natural processes, as it was here the Water of Leith flowed into it and deposited its sediment. Further to the west the loch was narrower and extended across much of what is now Carrick Knowe Golf Course with its southern margins almost reaching the railway line. Its western limit is now defined by Broomhouse Road.

It should be noted that this loch was formed on the site of a much older one. The first loch at Corstorphine was created as the glaciers retreated at the end of the last Ice Age, leaving deposits of boulder clay which blocked the route of the Water of Leith at Coltbridge, Roseburn. Behind this barrier a loch formed. A similar process took place further west as the course of the River Almond was also blocked, creating a large sheet of water at Turnhouse. The first loch at Corstorphine left deposits of grey silt with the remains of arctic flora and fauna. Excavations of these deposits have revealed the remains of elk, red deer and lemming. During this time there was another smaller loch at Hailes, where the park is today. As the glaciers retreated, deposits of sand and gravel were washed into these early lochs and partially filled in the hollows they occupied. The loch that existed in historical times was then formed. It in turn left behind evidence of its existence in the form of marl and peat deposits, being in places 12 to 19 feet deep (3.6 to 5.8m). The Water of Leith had managed to erode a passage through the deposits blocking its flow at Coltbridge by the time of the formation of the second loch.

The loch and marshland acted as a form of defence for Edinburgh from armies approaching from the west. The village of Corstorphine grew up on a site opposite a narrow strip of land which formed a crossing between Corstorphine and Gogar Lochs. Corstorphine is thought to take its name from Thorfin's crossing.

Between 1374 and 1405 a castle of considerable importance was built to guard this strategic crossing. The fortification was surrounded by a moat and could only be reached by means of a two-arched bridge. The castle's hundred-foot (30m) long curtain wall flanked by towers at either end overlooked the crossing. It was said to have been sacked and destroyed by Chancellor Crichton in 1443 and to have then been rebuilt, but there is no evidence for this. Although not large, the castle was in a strategic position, guarding the main route between the royal castles of Edinburgh and Stirling. Corstorphine Hill was to the north of the road and to the south was the castle flanked by lochs and marshy ground, making attacks difficult. That this position was important is shown by a map of Scotland made by John Hardyng, a spy for the English King Edward IV. This shows Corstorphine as one of the few strategic places between the Royal Burghs.

The Earl of Mar, Regent of Scotland, garrisoned the Castle in 1572 to prevent supplies reaching Kirkcaldy of Grange, then in control of Edinburgh Castle. It remained in use until the eighteenth century when it fell into disrepair, at about the same time Corstorphine Loch was drained. Today nothing remains of the castle which stood immediately to the south of Dovecot Road. The dovecote which stands in the road of the same name may, however, have been associated with the castle. This structure may owe its survival to supernatural protection and anyone demolishing it will die within a short time. Another earlier stronghold may have existed on the opposite bank of the loch at Broomhall, a short distance to the west. The medieval church located to the north of the former stronghold of the Forrester family also still stands today. The original settlement of Corstorphine was surrounded by water on three sides, Corstorphine Loch to the south and east and Gogar Loch to the west. The church served as a landmark to travellers negotiating the inhospitable marshland. It was the duty of a priest to place a burning lamp at the eastern end of the building to act as a beacon to those travelling after dark. The church received an endowment of land near Roseburn for providing this service, which became known as Lamp Acres. This guiding light for those traversing the land to the west of Edinburgh was first lit in 1429 and continued in operation for the next 350 years until it was extinguished in 1769. In 1958 a light was placed in the eastern end of Corstorphine Church to commemorate the oil-fired lamp once burned to guide travellers across the marshes.

When the field of Broomhouse, in what is now the Broomhall area, was being developed for housing in 1958/59, evidence of an old causeway was unearthed. In addition indications were found of a possible structure bridging the eastern end of Gogar Loch near Corstorphine. Despite the efforts to try to create causeways through the damp ground, provisions were still being conveyed from Coltbridge near Roseburn to Corstorphine by boat as late as 1633.

The loch, however, was partly drained and reclaimed in 1670, when a deep ditch known as the Stank was dug along its northern edge. Stank is a term derived from the French word l'étang meaning a pool, pond or slow-flowing ditch. A contemporary map dated 1680 shows the loch much reduced in size compared with the beginning of the same century. By 1763 most of it had disappeared, being converted into meadows and fields. The damp ground, however, continued to provide a source of reeds for thatching cottage roofs for another century. Peat was also dug from the margins of the former loch to supply Corstorphine village with fuel. When the loch existed water hemlock also grew in it. This plant is far more poisonous than the common hemlock.

It is only in the last two centuries that Edinburgh's suburbs have sprawled westwards across the site of Corstorphine Loch. Today the only surviving evidence of the largest of all the lochs formed in prehistoric times within Edinburgh is in the names of some of the streets. Lampacre, The Stank, Balgreen, Carrick Knowe all have connections with the former sheet of water, as does Corstorphine.

Gogar Loch

THIS LOCH WAS SEPARATED from Corstorphine Loch by a narrow strip of land which formed the crossing guarded by the castle. It is recorded that sometimes this narrow neck of land was flooded and passage across it was maintained by a ferry. Although Gogar Loch is referred to as a separate loch it originally must have been part of a larger Corstorphine Loch, becoming divided from the main body of water when the water levels dropped.

The Gogar Loch extended from Corstorphine Village in the east to the Edinburgh bypass in the west, covering most of the area now occupied

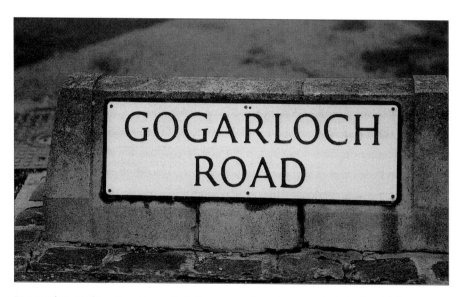

In several cases the only evidence that there was a long-forgotten loch in the vicinity is found in the street names. In 1982 a new road at the Gyle was called Gogarloch Road. This has been followed by Gogarloch Syke, Gogarloch Haugh and Muir which are all modern contrived creations. The Flashes or Flasshes in the same district is, however, a traditional name. It was the last part of Corstorphine Loch to survive before being drained in the late eighteenth century.

by the Gyle. The loch was around 1.5 miles in length and just under half a mile in breadth (0.8km). When combined with Corstorphine Loch, there would have been a continuous sheet of water from the site now occupied by the city centre to the western edge of Edinburgh. Gogar Loch in the last centuries of its life was likely to have been very shallow. The Gogar Burn flowed into the western end of the loch at a site where the Edinburgh Business Park now stands. A Bronze Age sword was discovered close to Gorgarburn House, possibly thrown into the water as an offering to the gods and possible evidence that the loch extended this far west. In the late twentieth century evidence of an Iron Age fort at Redheughs in the Edinburgh Business Park came to light. The name Redheughs is derived from the reddish-coloured soil and from an old word meaning 'the land rising beside a river'. This is proof that the land around Gogar Loch was far from devoid of human habitation in prehistoric times despite its low-lying nature and its associated marshy characteristics. The fort at Redheughs had many defensive ditches protecting it and like Corstorphine Castle it may have utilised the waterlogged ground to enhance its defences. Much of the area now occupied by Edinburgh Business Park was extensively occupied from the prehistoric to the Roman period. There was also a Bronze Age field system which is 3,000 to 4,000 years old. Perhaps its crops were watered from the nearby Gogar Loch. The very flat site occupied by Gogar Loch must have resulted in great variations in its size, as it expanded during periods of heavy rain and contracted in warm summers. In 1650 General Leslie entrenched his troops on what was perhaps the margin of the loch. Soldiers under the command of Oliver Cromwell tried to dislodge the Scottish troops from their position but the ground was so boggy that they had to be content with bombarding them with artillery. Cromwell was forced to beat a temporary retreat after this engagement, his plans thwarted by the muddy terrain! At this time some of the area appears to have been drained, as in 1661 James Forrester petitioned Parliament with a complaint that the Gogar Burn was overflowing into the surrounding fields and meadows due to the neglect of the ditches by those who formerly kept them clear.

By 1763, according to a map drawn at that time, Corstorphine Loch had just about disappeared while Gogar Loch still survived. Another map published ten years later, however, records its site as a marsh. Pools of water still survived at the western end site of the Gogar Loch and during the severe winter of 1794 were used to host a curling competition which lasted several days. Despite the digging of ditches, the New Statistical Account of Scotland recorded autumn flooding in the west meadow of the Gyle Muir in 1836 when 20 acres (8 hectares) became covered with water and was home to wildfowl. Even in 1960 30 acres (12 hectares) of marshland existed on the south side of the Glasgow Road with the area overgrown with rushes. Unfortunately it was reclaimed a year or so later. Several feet of pure peat were excavated at this location.

Other~ Prehistoric Lochs

Craigcrook Loch

THIS LOCH LAY ON THE eastern side of Corstorphine Hill. It was centred on what is now the junction of Craigcrook Road and March Road and the entire site of the former loch is now covered by houses. A small pond remained in the first half of the twentieth century but it too has succumbed to the spread of Edinburgh's suburbs. Craigcrook Loch does not seem to have been of any great extent. The alluvial deposits are not much more than ¼ mile (400m) in length. A small stream drained from this body of water, running eastwards along a hollow now occupied by Craigcrook Road. Remains of red deer have been recovered from the deposits left by the loch. The loch is shown as still being in existence on seventeenth-century maps but even then it was of limited extent and hardly amounts to more than a large pond. However much of the surrounding ground on the south side of the Queensferry Road was flat and possibly was flooded when the loch overflowed. Craigcrook Castle came into being in 1545 when it was a keep for the defence of Edinburgh in the event of a siege. It overlooked Craigcrook Loch and was surrounded by marshland which contributed to its protection. In more recent times marl was dug from the former site of the loch. Many of these workings had already become flooded by the eighteenth century. Some of the marl pits could still be seen in the first half of the twentieth century, although some is an old story that a horse and cart stumbled into one of the flooded pits and disappeared without trace!

Holyrood Abbey stands in the middle of an old loch basin. Remnants of the loch survived well into the Middle Ages. Elias, the tenth Abbot is recorded as having drained the marshes around 1224. He is said to have been buried under the high altar in the Lady Chapel.

Tributaries of the River Tumble flowed on either side of the Abbey, amalgamating a short distance to the east of it. Although the Abbey is alleged to have been founded in response to the divine intervention which saved King David I from being mauled to death by a stag he was hunting, this story only appeared in print a couple of centuries after the event. In 1924, excavations under the Abbey unearthed what was believed to be the remains of a Celtic church and part of a causeway although the discovery has in recent times been re-interpreted as being part of the Abbey. It would, however, have been the type of location favoured by the Celtic form of Christianity. Perhaps it is not stretching credibility to speculate that there may originally have been an early Christian church here, situated in the centre of a small loch reached by a causeway.

Holyrood Loch

THERE IS EVIDENCE THAT an extensive loch once existed at the foot of Edinburgh's Old Town. It occupied a glacial hollow at the base of Salisbury Crags and possibly extended as far as Meadowbank. The main body of water stretched north from the base of Salisbury Crags to Abbeyhill, a distance of just under ½ mile (800m) and from the Canongate in the west to Queens Park on the east. Holyrood Palace and Abbey were built in what would have been the middle of the loch. As the Abbey was founded in the twelfth century it would appear that much of the water had disappeared by then. The numerous streams flowing down the side of Arthur's Seat and Salisbury Crags would have deposited considerable quantities of mud and silt. There is some evidence however that Holyrood Loch had not completely disappeared by the Middle Ages, as there is a reference in the Lord High Treasurer's Accounts to the draining of the loch beside the Abbey for conversion into a garden in 1597. The Watergate, one of the entrances to the town, lay at the foot of the Canongate and close to Holyrood Abbey. Its name was derived from a large pool of water used for watering horses. Perhaps this was another relic of the former Holyrood Loch. As recently as the beginning of the nineteenth century much of the ground at the foot of Salisbury Crags is shown on contemporary plans as being damp and going by the name of the King's Meadow. Excavations of the site occupied by Holyrood Loch indicate it reached a depth of around 30–40 feet (9–12m) near Holyrood Palace. In its early history this sheet of water experienced numerous floods but as time progressed conditions became drier and more tranquil as evidenced by the remains of delicate mollusca which flourish in such conditions. In 1887 a cutting for a sewer was made near the Palace Gardens. The excavation went down to a depth of about twenty feet (6 metres) and revealed the following information. The first six feet (2 metres) near the surface consisted of deposits with fragments of pottery, oyster shells, bones, etc resting on brown peaty clay about a foot (0.3 metre) in thickeness. This bed continued down into peat, which had a depth of 1½ feet (½ metre). Underneath it was a layer of marl, 1–2 feet thick (0.3–0.6 metre). The lowest part of the section consisted of brown and blue clay resting on loose clayey sand which seems to have formed the floor of the loch. Rather appropriately when 'Our Dynamic Earth', a tourist attraction which relates the story of Scotland's geology, was under construction there was an echo of the long-forgotten loch. Large quantities of ground water were found to exist around 6½ feet (2m) below the surface, the remains of the 10,000-year-old sheet of water. The new Scottish Parliament opposite the 'Our Dynamic Earth' is on what was once an area deep under water!

Appropriately its landscaped grounds will include a number of ponds which unlike the ancient Holyrood Loch will not be static. A pumping system will cause the water to flow and froth to discourage birds from alighting here and causing a pollution hazard.

Hunters Bog

SITUATED IN A VALLEY between Arthur's Seat and Salisbury Crags is the site of another prehistoric loch. Its waters would have drained into the Holyrood Loch, which was situated only a few hundred yards away on lower ground to the north. Close to its long-vanished waters, evidence of prehistoric circular huts have been found and rank among the oldest archaeological remains discovered in Edinburgh. In medieval times, as with the Nor Loch, a dam was placed across the valley to control the drainage from Hunters Bog and provide power for a mill which ground grain for the monks of Holyrood Abbey. The mill pond seems to have disappeared by 1564 as it is said Mary Queen of Scots gave an instruction for an artificial loch to be again created in this valley, but for an entirely different purpose. A banquet was spread out on its edges to celebrate the marriage of one of her ladies in waiting. Model ships were used to create a miniature naval pageant based on the siege of Leith which had taken place in 1560. The bog was drained in the mid-nineteenth century and ditches dug to take water down to St Margaret's Loch. For the next hundred years the ground housed a number of rifle ranges. This activity ceased in 1961 and a small new pond was created in the late twentieth century to attract wildlife. A short distance to the north east are the stark remains of St Anthony's Chapel which date back to medieval times. At night a light was burned in this building to guide those foolhardy enough to travel after nightfall through the low marshy ground lying to the north of Arthur's Seat.

Blackford Loch

THIS IS ONE OF TWO possible prehistoric lochs that lay on the course of the Jordan Burn. Deposits of the former loch bed show that this feature was about ½ mile (800m) long at its maximum extent. It lay on the north-east side of Blackford Hill and today its limits are marked by West Savile

Terrace on the south, Relugus Road on the north, Blackford Avenue on the west and Mayfield Road to the east. It should not be confused with Blackford Pond which is a recent creation.

Jordan Burn Loch

THIS WAS SITUATED UPSTREAM of Blackford Loch at Morningside. It extended from Morningside Road westwards to the appropriately named Myreside Road. The latter is an indication that the area once occupied by this feature remained marshland into historical time taking its name from an area called the Common Myre. Early references also make mention of Merchiston Loch, the exact location of which is not known. It is perhaps a reference to the Jordan Loch. The area of marshland would have been overlooked by Merchiston Castle, a strong fifteenth-century keep, commanding the rising ground to the east.

Little France Loch

ALLUVIAL DEPOSITS ON THE banks of Burdiehouse Burn, between Little France and Niddrie, point to the existence of a prehistoric loch here. On a map dating from around 1650, the area is shown as being damp. Originally this area of marshland would have enhanced the defences of Craigmillar Castle which overlooks it. Some of the area must have dried out many centuries ago as the ancient settlement of Little France occupies the area where the Burdiehouse Burn would have flowed into the loch. The New Edinburgh Royal Infirmary stands on top of part of the former loch bed.

The Cowgate Loch (The South Loch)

ALLUVIAL DEPOSITS OF A limited extent are a possible indication that a loch or pond occupied a glacial hollow on the south side of the Castle rock. There was a local tradition that a loch once existed in this area and this was the original South Loch with the name later being transferred to the Burgh Loch on the site of the Meadows. 'Provinciae Edinburgenae Descriptio' written in 1647–1652 states that there was a loch here until it was drained in the first half of the fifteenth century. A tributary of the River Tummel flowed through the Cowgate. Its source was the south side of the Castle rock, it then rippled through the Grassmarket and down to the Cowgate and Holyrood, where it merged with the branch that flowed through the Nor Loch valley. Lord Cockburn in his book *Memorials* recalls that this stream, sometimes known as the Coogate Strand, 'when in flood was a great torrent, not filling the cellars merely, but almost the whole street.'

The Coogate Strand is now a sewer buried under the roadway, like most of the other Edinburgh streams.

Turnhouse Loch

OF ALL THE LOCHS THAT once existed in the Edinburgh area, this was the biggest but perhaps one of the shortest-lived. It was centred on the River Almond and covered the land now occupied by Edinburgh Airport and all its runways. At the end of the last Ice Age, the river flowed into the Firth of Forth about a mile north of its present position. Its route eastwards was blocked by a ridge of high ground that runs parallel to the A90 dual carriageway. Until the River Almond broke through the gorge at Craigiehall, near Cramond Bridge, a large loch built up behind this barrier. It seems to have disappeared by the Bronze Age as the Cat Stane, a standing stone from this period, occupies a site near the River Almond on what was the centre of the loch. Also a number of other prehistoric monuments have been found in the vicinity. A seventeenth-century description of the area, however, states that the River Almond often flooded the low-lying fields with great loss to the dwellers in the vicinity of its banks, especially in autumn. In 1843, a small loch known as Druid Loch could still be found at Newliston, at the western end of the bed of the former Turnhouse Loch. It may be responsible for giving Lochend Street its name. The site of Hallyards Castle is not far away. It was originally a stronghold of the Knights Templars and originally may have been surrounded by water or a marsh. Another possibility for the origin of the street name of Lochend is that it may take its name from a settlement shown on Pont's seventeenth-century map called Lochend situated beside a small body of water in the neighbourhood of Ratho. There was in fact another prehistoric loch, south-east of Ratho, its site now partly occupied by a golf course, and this may be the same feature shown on Pont's map.

Another area of lake alluvium is found between Colinton and Braidburn, including Redford. It may have been formed in a similar manner to that of the Turnhouse Loch, with the course of the Braidburn being initially blocked by glacial sand and gravel close to a point where Oxgangs Avenue crosses the stream today. Once the stream found its way through the deposit the loch drained away.

Ponds for the Public

THE PUBLIC PARK has its origins in the Victorian era. In response to increasing urbanisation and industrialisation, green spaces were estab﹐lished to counteract the unhealthy living conditions. Although Glasgow Green was Scotland's first urban park, dating from the mid﹐eighteenth century, most Scottish public parks were created after 1840. Ill﹐drained sites which were often beds of old glacial lochs or flood plains of rivers were favoured for parks. They could be purchased cheaply and had often escaped development as builders favoured the better﹐drained ground in the vicinity. In 1878 the Public Parks (Scotland) Act gave town councils the powers to purchase marginal lands for recreational purposes at low cost.

One of the oldest ponds in public grounds is that in the Royal Botanic Garden. It dates from around 1822 when the Botanic Garden was established on its current site at Inverleith. The crescent moon﹐shaped pond was created on an area of marshy ground. Today it still forms a central attraction in the gardens although it has been supplemented by a new water feature in an area featuring Chinese plants which was completed in the closing years of the twentieth century. Originally the Botanic Garden was situated at the head of the Nor Loch and then transferred to a site at the edge of the eighteenth﹐century town. Here, in the 1760s, a five﹐acre (2﹐hectare) garden was established with an oval pond being the central feature. Today this site has been built over and is now occupied by the tenements of Haddington Place forming part of Leith Walk.

Edinburgh's first Zoological Gardens were situated a short distance away from the Botanical Garden at Inverleith. Located in the grounds of a mansion house known as Broughton Park, which was found between East Claremont Street and what later became Bellevue Road, were enclosures for polar bears, wolves, hyenas and tigers. In the south﹐east corner there was as a pit with a pond. Contemporary illustrations show an unusual

St Margaret's Loch, Holyrood Park, Edinburgh. Although this loch is a Victorian creation it occupies a natural hollow which may have held a loch or marsh in medieval times.

assortment of birds resident here. There are native species such as swans and ducks rubbing necks with pelicans and other exotic birds. The zoo entertained the public from 1840 until it closed its doors in 1867. The pond and animal enclosures were built over in the late nineteenth century. In 1913 the Scottish National Zoological park was established on Corstorphine Hill. Quarries opened for the construction of the roads for the zoo were converted into pools and animal enclosures. Local streams running down the side of Corstorphine Hill supply water for the numerous artificial ponds. The zoo is one of Scotland's most popular tourist attractions.

Holyrood Park has been a royal park for many centuries. Such parks were not originally for the benefit of the general public but were the exclusive preserve of the monarch to carry out his pursuits particularly that of hunting. By the late eighteenth century, however, Holyrood Park was being used by Edinburgh's citizens in increasing numbers. Prince Albert, in 1844, drew up plans to improve the grounds and make them more accessible to the public. Among his ideas were the creation of artificial lochs and the road through the park which became known as Queen's Drive. The first man-made body of water to be created was Dunsapie Loch on the eastern slopes of Arthur's Seat, where there was already a marsh. In the Middle Ages the monks of the nearby St Anthony's chapel had a fish pond at this location. Although the loch was created by placing a dam at its tail, a 1817 map already refers to the marsh here as Dunsapie Loch. The loch occupies a crescent-shaped hollow and is around 750 feet in length (228m). During 1745 part of Prince Charlie's army camped on the hillside overlooking the present site of the loch. In 1862 only a few years after Dunsapie Loch had been created there was a proposal to build a restaurant in the form of a rustic cottage adjacent to it. This plan met with such hostile public opinion that the idea was dropped.

During the early years of the twentieth century the loch was used by skaters but now it is the exclusive domain of ducks and geese.

St Margaret's Loch was made a few years after Dunsapie Loch, being completed around 1857. Like the other loch it is situated in a marshy area gouged out by the ice. In prehistoric times it may well have been part of Holyrood Loch indicated by traces of alluvial deposits on the site. St Margaret's Loch was originally known as St Anthony's Loch and is around 695 feet long (211m) and 290 feet wide (88m). It is supplied by water from the nearby Hunters Bog further up the hill. It is believed that King David had his legendary encounter with the stag he was hunting somewhere around where the loch is situated today. In the forest that covered the area in the twelfth century, the King became separated from his hunting companions and was unhorsed by a large stag. The stag was about to attack the King when a miracle happened. The creature suddenly ran off at the sight of the 'True Cross' which mysteriously appeared in the King's hands. King David founded the nearby Abbey of Holyrood in gratitude of the miraculous divine intervention, according to legend.

The deer have long since disappeared but St Margaret's Loch hosts a large variety of bird life. The loch is a favourite wintering location for swans. Up to the 1960s the resident bird life had to compete with rowing boats that were hired to the public in the summer months. A large paddling pool for children was constructed at the side of the loch in 1950 but is no more. The depth of the loch is less than 5 feet (1½m).

The first ponds that were constructed in public parks managed by the Council were at Inverleith and Blackford. The land on which Inverleith Pond is situated was acquired for public use in 1896 and in the same year the area was banked around and flooded to form this sheet of water. In 1908 it was stated that the pond was most expensive and troublesome to maintain owing to the excessive amount of weed on the bottom. During 1959 the bottom was covered with special gravel to restrict the growth of weed which was interfering with the sailing of model yachts and boats. This hobby has been practised here since the formation of the pond and is the only body of water in Edinburgh set aside for this pastime. Originally the pond was four to five feet deep (1.2–1.7m) but in the 1960s it was partially filled in with broken rocks to make it shallower for safety reasons. Swans, which were common in the early part of the twentieth century, have returned to winter here in large numbers in the closing years of the twentieth century after a long absence. Blackford Pond has existed in its present form from around 1908 when the ground was acquired for public use. In the nineteenth century there was a curling pond on the site. It was the home ground to the Waverley Curling Club established in 1848. By 1896 only a very small rectangular pond was left on the site of Blackford Pond with the rest of the area being open ground. The current pond is only three to four feet (1m) deep although when it was created it is thought to have been around twelve feet (3.6m) deep. It is fed by springs running off Blackford Hill. Up until the 1960s it was a popular location for skating once its waters had frozen over. Sometimes the pond was floodlit by gas flares for skating in the dark winter evenings. It is now home to mallard, tufted ducks and moorhens. Greylag geese from Duddingston Loch are frequent visitors.

Figgate Park on the east side of Edinburgh, with its pond, was opened in 1938. The park's construction commenced in 1936 on the site of former clay pits which once supplied the nearby potteries of Portobello with raw material. An island was created in the middle of the pond with the intention of it becoming a small bird sanctuary. Extensive improvements were carried out to the park in the late 1990s.

Straiton Pond is situated next to the Edinburgh bypass and close to Straiton Retail Park. It was also created on old clay pits. Between 1855 and 1894 blue clay was dug from the workings to supply Clippen Brick Works. Extraction ceased during 1952 and in 1982 a nature reserve was established

Inverleith Pond, Inverleith Park, Edinburgh. Swans have been kept on Edinburgh's lochs and ponds for ornamental purposes since the sixteenth century.

by Edinburgh District Council. In 1996 ownership passed to Midlothian Council with the reorganisation of local government. The pond is 850 ft (260m) long and 130–190 ft (40–60m) wide. Unlike many of the above ponds the water is very deep! The pond attracts birds like moorhen, coot, dabchick and occasionally grey herons.

On the north-west side of Craiglockhart Hill lies Craiglockhart Pond. Now in public ownership, it was originally created in 1873 by John Cox as a boating, curling and skating pond for use by Edinburgh's citizens. The pond occupies a glacial hollow like that at Blackford. Prior to the creation of the artificial pond the area was meadowland, although in prehistoric times there may well have been a natural pond in the vicinity. One theory concerning the origin of the name Craiglockhart is that it derives from the 'high craig by the loch', on the basis that Corstorphine Loch once extended up to its base. It is unlikely that this loch ever extended this far south in historic times. The generally accepted explanation of the name is that it originates from the name of the family that once owned the land here. In the late nineteenth century the newly created sheet of water had the rather unusual name Craiglockhart Safety Pond. During 1976 a new sports centre opened next to Craiglockhart Pond, a special feature of which is the facilities for water sports. Fairmilehead Park off Comiston Road is a relatively recent park only coming into city ownership in 1964. It has a small pond on the north side caused by the damming of a small steam.

Although no new ponds have been created in public parks for many years, the city of Edinburgh, in conjunction with private enterprise, has executed a major new water feature at the Edinburgh Business Park at the Gyle. A series of ponds was created by damming the Gogar Burn to form an attractive landscaped area in the centre of a major office development. The first of the two ponds, or lochs as they are called, was completed in 1993 and covered around 1.5 acres (0.6 hectare). It is called Loch Craig after the founder of Edinburgh's New Town. Forget-me-nots, water lilies and marsh marigolds are planted round its sides. Despite it being overlooked by office blocks, swans and ducks have made it their home. The second loch was created in the closing years of the twentieth century and is named after the late Bill Ross who was responsible for its formation and the stylish layout of the Edinburgh Park. Rather appropriately these bodies of water have been created on what was once the western end of the now drained Gogar Loch! Perhaps the pinnacle of evolution of the pond as a recreation feature was reached in 2002. A structure consisting of a huge S-shaped landform, rising to 20 feet (7 metres) with three crescent-shaped pools, was completed in the grounds of the Scottish National Gallery of Modern Art. The earthworks and pools of water are to be used as 'a setting for outdoor sculpture' as well as being claimed to be a work of art themselves. The feature was created by Charles Jencks, a US architectural historian.

Curling and Skating Ponds

IN BYGONE CENTURIES these outdoor activities were far more popular than they are today. Curling was virtually a national pastime in the nineteenth century, being played the length and breadth of Scotland. It was played on Canonmills Loch and the Nor Loch before they were drained and more recently on Duddingston Loch. In 1829 it is recorded that Corstorphine Curling Club meetings took place anywhere as soon as an area of marsh or water froze. Later in the century they created a permanent pond from a small steam, possibly the Bughtlin Burn, on the Estate of Clermiston. This club is recorded as playing competitions at Murrayburn, Millburn and Kiershill, the latter a large pond near the Calder Road. The makeshift curling venues gave way to more permanent ponds that were constructed across Edinburgh in the second half of the nineteenth century. Much effort went into creating curling ponds and thereafter keeping them in as good condition as possible. Their bottoms had to be mown during the summer so that when the water was put in at the beginning of November the grass did not show above! Burrowing animals, through whose holes in the banking all the water could run out, had to be dealt with and leaking sluices made watertight.

One of the first artificial curling ponds in the Edinburgh area was constructed on Harlaw Moor, about one mile east of Balerno at 'about the height of Arthur's Seat'. It went by the name of Col. Scott's Pond. When Craiglockhart Pond was built, a curling pond was also created on its southern edge. There was a large curling pond on the north side of the Meadows where Lonsdale Terrace stands today. A curling pond also existed a short distance to the north of Fettes College and another close to the railway line at Morningside. When Blackford Pond was created in the early twentieth century on the site of an old curling pond, a new one was created for this sport immediately to the west of it. Other locations with curling ponds in use around the same time included Bellevue Terrace where there were new tarmac ponds, a cement pond at Perth Street, Lochrin Ice Pond and at Slateford where there was both a natural pond and two artificial ones. In 1907, four tarmac rinks were constructed at Pinkhill, near Edinburgh Zoo, but were abandoned in 1914. On the south side of Duddingston Loch there are still the remains of two lochside rinks

A man-made water feature created in the late twenteith century at the Edinburgh Business Park. It sits on an area once occupied by the Gogar Loch.

which were flooded and left to freeze when conditions on the loch itself were unsafe for this sport. Duddingston Curling Society was finally disbanded in 1948.

Today most of the curling ponds have disappeared although the sport is still practised indoors at Gogar Park Curling Club near the Glasgow Road. One reason for the decline of the sport appears to have been the lack of freezing conditions to create ice on ponds. Interestingly Corstorphine Curling club decided to transfer their activities to an indoor ice rink for the 1918–19 season as the climate had, according to them, become less favourable for the sport! Skating, like curling, could be practised on a few inches of frozen water. Duddingston Loch had been the favourite venue for this activity in the eighteenth and nineteenth centuries. In the early years of the twentieth century most of the ponds in the public parks were criss-crossed by the lines left by skates once the water had frozen. A large skating pond was created on the Braids Golf Course around the beginning of the twentieth century. The long dry bed of this pond is still visible, close to the old cart track and not far from the Howe of Dean pathway that descends down to the Braid Burn. This would be the first venue in the Edinburgh area to have ice that could bear the weight of the skaters, due to its altitude and exposed situation. It was probably for this reason the skating pond was constructed in this relatively remote location. On the opposite side of the golf course, near its highest point, existed a small seasonal pool known as Deidman's Pool. It was little more than a small marshy area and often dries up completely. At the beginning of the twenty-first century a small manmade pond was constructed on the eastern edge of Deidman's Pool which will give this feature a sense of permanency. There was also a curling pond a short distance from the Braids on the site now occupied by Mortonhall Tennis club. It existed from 1890 to 1914.

Lochs and Ponds for Country Houses

L ONG BEFORE landscaped areas were created for the use of the general public, country houses in the vicinity of Edinburgh were surrounded by large gardens and areas of parkland set aside for the exclusive use of their owners. As improvements took place in agriculture and landowners' income grew, they built new country houses, or in the Lothian area often adapted and extended their traditional fortified houses. Up until the mid-eighteenth century most gardens were geometric in form and this was reflected in the shape of the ponds, which were usually rectangular and often referred to as canals. A major change in style occurred in the second half of the century when natural landscapes consisting of grass and scattered indigenous trees became fashionable. The design often included a serpentine pond. Almost all the artificial lochs and ponds created in the grounds of country and mansion houses in the vicinity of Edinburgh date from the eighteenth or early nineteenth centuries. An exception to this was Craigmillar Castle which had a terraced garden laid out in the sixteenth century, when the Prestons controlled the castle. Their coat of arms is engraved over the gateway to the outer courtyard. Immediately south of the ruined castle walls is the outline of a fish pond in the shape of a P. As well as enhancing the grounds of their residence, the fish pond had a more functional role which was that of providing fresh food. The long-vanished Corstorphine Castle also had a fish pond within its grounds. A large fish pond of a more recent era, however, still exists south of Castle Craig, in the grounds of Dalmeny House. It was created out of an area of bog in the second half of the nineteenth century

Several examples of water features created in the early eighteenth century, when gardens were laid out to a geometric pattern, survive within the city of Edinburgh's boundaries. It should be noted that many of the gardens listed below are still on private estates and are not generally accessible. Some of them do have open days when the public are allowed to enter the grounds.

Newliston House, situated to the west of Edinburgh, near Kirkliston, has a spectacular landscaped garden. It was laid out between 1722 and 1744 by a reputed force of 200 workmen to a plan drawn up by William Adam. The 2nd Earl of Stair who inherited the property was the ambassador at the Palace of Versailles, which inspired him to create a formal French style of garden complete with cascades, canals, ponds, terraces and serpentine walks at Newliston. Much of the landscape survives to this day including a canal type pond which bisects it. In the centre of the canal feature is a half moon shaped pond. The classical villa interestingly was built after the landscape had been created and lies immediately to the south of the canal.

Drum House, on the southern edge of Edinburgh was built between 1726 and 1734. Like Newliston House its grounds were designed by William Adam. There is a long canal pond to the east of the house, parallel to the west east avenue. In the closing decades of the twentieth century it had become silted up. A canal type pond was constructed between 1724 and 1740, a short distance from the site of the now ruined seventeenth century Cammo House. Once it was used for curling but now the grounds of the house are a public park. It was at Cammo House in the early eighteenth century that the first attempt to create a landscaped garden in Scotland was made by its then owner, Sir John Clerk of Penicuik.

Dalmahoy House, lying south east of Ratho, was another William Adam design, this time for the youngest son of the Earl of Stair. It was finished in 1725. The grounds were laid out to a formal pattern but unlike those at nearby Newliston House were swept away by the Earl of Morton who purchased the estate in 1750. He favoured the new fashion of creating a 'natural landscape', a movement made popular by Capability Brown, the English landscape designer. At Dalmahoy, the avenue to the east was felled and replaced by a large pond which still exists today. This resembles a natural feature, unlike the previously mentioned examples. Walks were created that meandered past the pond or loch as it was sometimes referred to and led to the woodland beyond. Lime trees dating from the eighteenth century could still be found on the north side of the loch in the late twentieth century. Also on Dalmahoy Estate is Kiershill Pond, sometimes known as Crow Wood Pond. Unlike the other loch this is a natural pond enlarged to host curling competitions which were frequently held here in the nineteenth century. By late twentieth century its main function was as a wildlife reserve.

Although Riccarton House, a sixteenth-century tower with a Jacobean extension, was demolished in 1956 its pond still survives. Heriot Watt University took over the site in 1967 and developed a new campus here. The pond, which goes by the name of Fire Pond and dates from the eighteenth century, is located next to the library. (The ponds of country houses often had a functional role, namely that of supplying water for fire fighting.) A larger pond known as the 'loch' was constructed in the early 1970s by the university as a centrepiece for the new campus.

Craigiehall House has a pond which is much neglected. The pond is situated close to the A90 road just beyond Cramond Bridge and there is no public access. Dating from 1699, it was army headquarters for Scotland in the late twentieth century.

Several major water features have totally vanished in the last 150 years or so. The most impressive were those at Duddingston House. The Earl of Abercorn purchased the estate of Duddingston in 1745 with the intention of establishing it as a place of residence as he had several Scottish titles but no land in Scotland. Rather surprisingly the grounds were laid out a decade or so before the house was built. Some 200 acres (80 hectares) of what was once farmland were fenced off and transformed into one of Scotland's most impressive gardens which included features such as small lochs, cascades, grottoes, temples and statues. The series of lochs and ponds was created by damming the Braid Burn whose course was also altered to sweep round the house in a semi-circle. The largest loch situated on the north side of the house was almost as big as Lochend Loch is today. In the centre of it there was even an island, known as Crow Island, complete with a clump of trees and rookery. The chain of lochs and ponds on the opposite side of the house stretched for about 700 yds (640m). The magnificent classical house constructed between 1763 and 1767 fortunately survives today but other than the stream itself all the water features had disappeared by the end of the nineteenth century. By this time the owners rarely stayed in their property and the grounds became neglected. They were eventually taken over by Duddingston Golf Course and a recent small pond occupies the low area between the mansion house and the columnar domed temple where the largest loch once was. When the ponds and lochs existed they were sometimes used by curlers from Duddingston Loch when it became too crowded for them there.

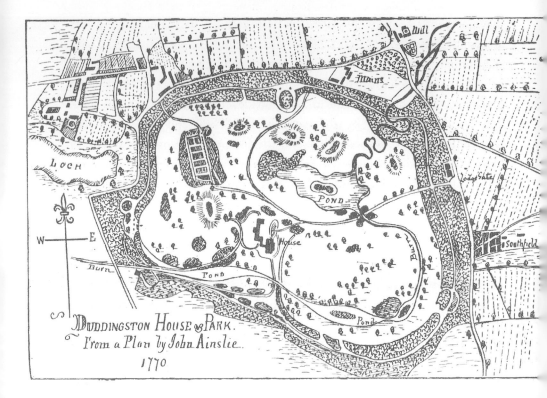

DUDDINGSTON HOUSE & PARK.
From a Plan by John Ainslie.
1770

This plan shows the complex of water features that existed in the grounds of Duddingston House, shortly after it was completed. Numerous other mansion houses in and around Edinburgh at the end of the eighteenth and early nineteenth century also had large ponds but none could rival those of Duddingston House for size or complexity. They were referred to in a book called *The Beauties of Scotland*, published in 1824. 'This villa, with pleasure grounds or park which have been annexed to it, exhibits an example of all that money or art can do to adorn a nearly flat surface, through which a small stream of water naturally runs with clumps, groves, canals, lakes, isles, cascades, temples, shrubbery, serpentine walks and spreading lawns'.
   Note that Duddingston Loch sits on western edge of the grounds of Duddingston House.

   Cameron House near Cameron Toll once boasted a serpentine pond around 100 yds long (91m). The pond had disappeared by the late nineteenth century although the building survives surrounded by twentieth-century houses. Other ornamental water features which have since disappeared include a pond in the grounds of the now demolished Niddrie House. It was in the vicinity of Niddrie House Avenue. An 1817 map also shows a pond in the grounds of Falconhall House at Morningside. Close by in what is now the grounds of Ainslie Hospital was St Roque's House. It boasted a large serpentine pond complete with its own islands. This feature, however, had disappeared by the late nineteenth century.

Warriston House on the north side of Edinburgh and immediately east of the Botanic Gardens had a long, naturally shaped pond with an island at its western end. The length of the body of water was around 200 yards (182m). The pond had disappeared by 1832. The area which it occupied is still an open space and is now a sports ground. When it existed the pond would have stretched almost the full distance of the playing fields from Inverleith Row to Warriston Crescent. In the same area was Redbraes House whose grounds were said to be unsurpassed in Scotland in the early nineteenth century. Holes were cut in its hedge so passers-by could catch a glimpse of its charms. Its pond, created out of a natural bog, was situated close to the Water of Leith and had two small islands in it. There was an attempt to turn the garden into a public amusement park along the lines of Vauxhall Gardens in London, decorating it with statues and floodlighting. It was also known by the rather exotic name of the Mount Vesuvius Grounds and its pond was used in the late nineteenth century by the Edinburgh Skating Club. By the early twentieth century the gardens had been levelled. The site is now occupied by a rather insignificant Redbraes public park.

Baron Norton's property, situated on the eastern edge of Calton Hill, had a landscaped pond. It was located on the northern side of London Road close to the junction with Montrose Terrace. It disappeared around the middle of the nineteenth century as new houses spread outwards from the then expanding city. Another much larger pond could be found in the grounds of North Merchiston House. An 1817 map shows this feature to be over 200 yds long and 50 yds wide (180m by 45m) at its greatest breadth. The pond was cut in two with the construction of the Union Canal. The northern part of this body of water survived until the latter part of the nineteenth century. By 1877 it had been converted into large curling ponds with its irregular banks being reworked into straight lines. The western end of Watson Crescent now stands on the site of the pond.

Much further to the west stands Millburn Tower. The house, situated next to the former grounds of Gogarburn Hospital, was constructed in the early years of the nineteenth century. In 1805 Captain George Parkyns designed an American garden for Lady Lister in which two ponds were a feature. The house survives today but the ponds, one on the north side of the house and the other on the south side, had become silted up by the 1980s and have since disappeared.

Dundas Loch, also situated on the west side of Edinburgh close to South Queensferry, is the largest of all the ornamental bodies of water to have existed in the vicinity of the city. The loch is found in the grounds of Dundas Castle. It is shown on the seventeenth century map of Lothian by Timothy Pont and on later maps it is sometimes named Lily Loch. There is reference in the New Statistical Account, 1843, to a loch in the vicinity of Dundas Hill being recently drained, presumably Dundas Loch. Several oak trees in an excellent state of preservation were uncovered when the bed of the loch was exposed. In the nineteenth century quarrying was carried close to the site of the loch. Around 1900 Dundas Loch, which appears to have been reinstated a few decades after it was drained, was extended by artificial means and made into a pleasure and wildlife area. It is around 500 yards in length (457m). There is no public access to the loch. In 2003, a new pond was created on Dundas estate close to a disused curling pond inhabited by around sixty newts. It is the only known breeding site for the Great Crested Newt in the Edinburgh area. It was hoped the new pond which measures 645 square feet (60 square metres) and is around three feet in depth (one metre) would encourage the newts to spread. Only one other large scale pond has been built in recent years in the Edinburgh area to encourage amphibians, at Meadow Yard in Craigentinny.

In contrast to Dundas Loch a small pond can be found in Queen Street Gardens in the centre of Edinburgh. Despite being in the New Town and a short distance away from Princes Street, few persons have set eyes on it as the Gardens are only accessible to householders in the neighbouring street. The significance of the small man-made pond complete with its own island should not be underestimated. In the mid-nineteenth century, Robert Louis Stevenson spent his childhood years playing around this pond and sailing model boats on it. It is believed to have inspired the author to write his epic novel *Treasure Island.*

Canals and Canal Basins

AT THE BEGINNING of the twenty-first century, a large stone relief of a horse pulling a canal barge overlooks the busy thoroughfare of Lothian Road. Few of the passers-by on the street below realise that it is there. It serves as the only reminder of the extensive inland port that once existed on this site. Anyone travelling down Lothian Road in the late 1820s would have encountered bustling quays and numerous canal barges discharging their cargoes. The well-known landmark, the ABC Cinema, stood until the end of the twentieth century on what was the northern limit of Port Hopetoun Canal Basin. There is still a cinema here but it has been renamed the Odeon.

Port Hopetoun was the biggest of three basins which marked the eastern end of the Union Canal. It occupied the site between Lothian Road in the east and Semple Street to the west. Morrison Street marked its northern edge and Fountainbridge its southern limit. The canal was conceived in the closing years of the eighteenth century but construction was held up due to the wars with France, which was then ruled by Napoleon. The canal opened in 1822 and Port Hopetoun quickly became a focus for economic activity in what was then open countryside. It was 31½ miles long (51km), 5 feet deep (1.5 metres), 37 feet wide at the surface (11 metres) and 20 feet (6 metres) wide at the bottom. The main water supply came from Cobbinshaw Reservoir in the Pentlands. It descended via Bog Burn into the River Almond and then was taken near Midcalder into a feeder which met the canal just east of the Almond Aqueduct. Initially stables, cellars, overseers' houses and shelters for canal passengers were constructed around the canal basin. In a short time it was found necessary to dig a second canal basin which was given the name Port Hamilton after the Duke of Hamilton, who had a major interest in the Scottish coal mining industry. The basin was a narrow rectangular shape and situated a short distance to the west of Port Hopetoun. Along its sides were stored vast

The Union Canal, Viewforth, Edinburgh, close to the canal terminus.

amounts of coal transported from the coalfields of central Scotland to Edinburgh. The site is now partially occupied by the huge Scottish Widows office complex. A third canal basin, which is also no more, was constructed next to the former Lochrin Distillery.

As the canal trade boomed, further buildings were erected around Port Hopetoun. They included warehouses and a 'fine large building for the luggage boat companies' on the square where the passengers landed. It was possible to board a barge near Lothian Road and be conveyed to Glasgow on it, the journey taking around fourteen hours. In 2003 a similar journey by train took around forty-five minutes. On the main passenger services, efforts were made to reduce travelling time and notices were put up warning the public that the horses pulling the boat travelled 'at great speed' and it was therefore unsafe to walk on the towpath. In the spring and summer of 1835 six passenger boats a day were leaving Port Hopetoun for Glasgow. For a time there was also a night service for goods and passengers which commenced in 1833.

The first passage boat for the canal was built a short distance from it in Lochrin, behind Gilmore Place. Initially twelve passage boats were constructed for use on the canal in 1822, all made of wood. The Forth &

Clyde Company originally had strongly recommended the adoption of iron boats as these were more durable and easier to load than wooden ones. The company also looked to Holland for guidance, the clerk being instructed to obtain plans of the latest and most approved Dutch boats and to have regulations for their services translated. In addition to boats being constructed close to the banks of the canal at Tolcross others were assembled at shipyards in Leith.

The building of the railways in the 1840s brought the short-lived canal boom to an end. The canal basins lingered on until the early years of the twentieth century by which time traffic had dwindled to a handful of boats a year. The final death knell came when the slaughterhouses moved from Fountainbridge to Gorgie. The canal basins of Port Hamilton and Port Hopetoun were declared redundant and in 1921 were drained of water. The canal continued to function, truncated at Lochrin, for a few more years. Ironically the canal basins were used to supply water to the steam locomotives at Haymarket and Waverley Stations, and a new water pipe had to be laid to service their huge demand for water when the canal basins were filled in. Port Hopetoun was built over in 1935–36 with Lothian House, a huge art deco building occupying most of the former site of the canal basin. The stone relief commemorating Port Hopetoun is situated in the centre of the block. There were plans to revive the basin at Port Hamilton in the late 1980s as a centrepiece for a large office development. When Scottish Widows built their headquarters a decade later the idea of reinstating the canal basin had been dropped. Although the Union Canal is being restored to its past glory in the early years of the twenty-first century it had rather a low-key end in Edinburgh, tucked out of sight at the back of the brewery at Fountainbridge. In 2004, it was declared that the brewery would close bringing an end the last vestiges of industry on the banks of the waterway. A plan, however, was announced to use the canal as the focal piece for the regeneration of this quarter of Edinburgh. The amount of water space would be expanded and the canal would be extended into adjacent sites to provide more mooring and turning facilities for boats. Canal-side shops and cafes would be built to create a vibrant canal quarter.

As mentioned elsewhere it was intended to extend the canal to Leith through the site now occupied by Princes Street Gardens. Had this proposal been realised the Union Canal would have descended down to the city centre via a series of locks and basins parallel to Lothian Road. A basin would also have been constructed on the south side of St Cuthbert's Church. Several routes were proposed for continuing the waterway from Princes Street Gardens to Leith. One would have taken the canal round the base of Calton Hill and then to the sea by a route now occupied by Easter Road. The canal would have then bisected Leith Links before reaching the Firth of Forth. The grandfather of Robert Louis Stevenson was involved in one of these schemes. His proposed route would have bypassed the city centre, taking a route that went north from Dalry to the Dean Village and then eastwards to Leith skirting the northern edge of the New Town. The canal would have gone through Canonmills and Powderhall, descending down fourteen locks to the sea. He also intended to turn the site of the former Nor Loch into an elaborate inner city loch of great beauty to enhance the appearance of Edinburgh.

A lesser-known extension planned for the Union Canal which also came to nothing was the creation of a branch from Port Hopetoun to the eastern edge of Meadows. The route proposed by Hugh Baird, engineer in charge of building the Forth Clyde Canal and the Union Canal, would have taken the waterway across the heart of Tolcross to the northern perimeter of the Meadows. The canal would have continued along the northern edge of the Meadows and terminated at a basin close to the children's playground at the eastern end of the park, next to Buccleuch Street. This was not the first plan to involve a canal basin being built in the Meadows. Mr Rennie, a London engineer, suggested in the closing years of the eighteenth century that the route for the proposed Union Canal should enter Edinburgh via a canal basin on Bruntsfield Links. The canal would then descend to the Meadows by a series of locks on the Links. The city authorities objected to the proposed violation of an area set aside for recreational purposes, and hence these plans never materialised. The Union Canal never progressed any further east than the basins next to Lothian Road.

Edinburgh's Water~ Supply and Reservoirs

ALTHOUGH RUNNING WATER from a tap is considered a necessity of modern life, it was only in the latter part of the nineteenth century that many homes in Edinburgh came to possess this facility.

Rather surprisingly, despite being surrounded by numerous lochs, marshes and ponds in the sixteenth century, the 10,000 inhabitants of the city often suffered from water shortages. Within the medieval walls the main source of water was from pump wells, many of which were situated in the Cowgate. This was augmented by supplies from the Burgh Loch, whose site is now occupied by the Meadows Park and from nearby springs and streams. The use of baths was not encouraged due to the demand it placed on the water supply. In 1572 and 1582 water shortages prompted the magistrates to ban brewers from using the city's wells and instructed them to take water from the Burgh Loch. By the end of the sixteenth century this body of water was being used for a variety of unhygienic practices including the washing of linen and watering herds of cattle, and it was becoming increasingly shallow and silted up. There were large numbers of springs of 'sweet water', as it was referred to in contemporary documents, in the hills surrounding Edinburgh. The main problem was transporting sufficient quantities to where the people lived. Water carriers brought barrels of fresh water on foot from the Wells of Wearie, at the foot of Arthur's Seat and nearby streams. In 1616 Comiston springs were surveyed as a potential supply of fresh water.

After a long delay and perhaps prompted by a bad drought in 1653–54, the Town Council contracted a German engineer to construct a lead pipeline of around 3.5 miles (5.6km) in length to transport the water to the town. A large cistern was built on Castlehill, a short distance from the Nor Loch, and the first water flowed down the pipe about 1676. The cistern was about 60 feet (18m) lower than the springs and water flowed down the pipe propelled by gravity alone. Edinburgh was one of the first towns in Britain to have this type of water supply. It should be noted that to this day almost all of Edinburgh except Fairmilehead is supplied by water delivered solely by the power of gravity. The cistern at Castlehill supplied water to five wells allocated in the High Street, and a further nine outlets at other locations were added a short time later. Five of the original 1680s wells can still be seen, and one of them located close to John Knox's house was restored to working order in 1997.

To increase the supply further, water was brought to the reservoir on Castlehill from Tod's Well by a tunnel cut through rock. Further pipes were laid to Swanston Springs in 1760 but demand for water was increasing rapidly with the construction of the New Town. Both Comiston and Swanston springs, however, continued to supply water for Edinburgh until the twentieth century. Comiston springs were discontinued as a source for water in 1946 because of the danger of contamination from new houses being built in the area. The collecting cistern for the spring water still remains in open ground to the west of Swan Spring Avenue. The wellheads were each named after animals or birds and were marked with an appropriate lead sculpture of the creature. They were situated in and around the grounds of Hunter's Tryst School, their sites now marked by protective masonry.

The Swanston springs did not yield a great amount of water and tended to fail at the same time as the wells in the Old Town. From the sixteenth to mid-nineteenth centuries, all the new projects to increase the water supply appear to have been executed in response to drought and serious water shortages. There was often a long gap between the shortage and the appropriate action taken to remedy it! The Council was frequently short of money and there were disputes with the landowners who controlled the sources of the springs. In 1785 the first steps were taken to create Edinburgh's first reservoirs on the Pentland Hills at Bonaly.

It was decided to construct two reservoirs on a stretch of hollow ground partly occupied by the present Bonaly Reservoir. A pipe was laid from the lower one in a north-easterly direction to join the Swanston pipe. The Bonaly springs were abandoned when the Crawley springs began to supply water. During 1814, it was suggested that the proposed Union Canal could also be used as a means of supplying Edinburgh with water. The magistrates turned down this offer from the company intending building the canal stating that the canal water would be contaminated with 'filth poured in from crowded passage boats'. Two years later the magistrates reversed their decision and had to refute their suggestions that the water would be undrinkable by explaining that their plan would include a feeder of fresh water from the River Almond. An act of Parliament was passed in 1819 to collect water from this source and a section of Glencorse Burn. Glencorse Reservoir was constructed, lying in the northern part of the Pentland Hills, just outside the current City of Edinburgh boundary. The main function of this first major reservoir for the city was not, however, to supply it with drinking water. Rather, it served the role of ensuring that the Glencorse Burn and the River Esk had an adequate supply of water the year round. With the springs supplying water to these rivers being siphoned off as the main source of drinking water, there was the possibility that the watercourses could run dry in the summer months. Many industries such as paper-making depended on mill wheels for power and if the rivers fell below a certain level they could not continue in business. Glencorse was the first of what are known as compensation reservoirs to be completed in the Pentland Hills. This reservoir was constructed by three great engineers – Thomas Telford, John Rennie and James Jardine. The embankment was one of the earliest earth dams to be constructed in Britain and was a showpiece of its time, being visited by many continental engineers. St Catherine's Chapel that stood by the side of the old drove road was flooded but when there is a drought and the water levels fall, its alleged remains become visible. However, they amount to no more than a pile of stones.

In 1847 plans were put into action to raise the embankment of this reservoir. Once this work was complete its role was extended to that of supplying water as well. In the twenty-first century its main role is to act as a service reservoir for the Talla Aqueduct supply. Its capacity is 368 million gallons (1,673 million litres) and surface area 52 acres (21 hectares). The maximum depth is 72 feet (22m). Around the same time another reservoir was constructed above it, namely Loganlea with a capacity of 117 million gallons (532 million litres) and depth of 50 feet (15.5m).

In the late 1840s several other major reservoirs were constructed a short distance from Glencorse. It is probably no coincidence that a large number of reservoirs were built shortly after a major water shortage in 1847, when the Edinburgh Water Company appealed to owners of private wells to augment the city's dwindling supply.

The reservoirs were built on the northern edge of the Pentland Hills to exploit the 250-plus springs that flow from this area. With the draining of Corstorphine and Gogar lochs in the seventeenth and eighteenth centuries, Edinburgh had no large bodies of fresh water in its vicinity until the reservoirs were built. Some of the springs that emerge from the northern edge of the Pentland Hills flow into the River Almond but most are in the Water of Leith catchment area. The spring water is taken by an underground aqueduct from the collecting area to Edinburgh a few miles away. To maintain a regular supply of water three reservoirs were built: Clubbiedean, Torduff and Bonaly. The latter replaced the earlier two reservoirs constructed here in the previous century. Today the reservoir reconstructed in 1853 at Bonaly is only used for compensation purposes. It has a surface area when full of 14.5 acres (5.9 hectares) and a capacity of 44 million gallons (200 million litres). Its maximum depth is just over 22 feet (7m). Torduff Reservoir occupies a valley that was formed by melting water in the last stages of the Ice Age. The reservoir dates from 1851 and has a surface area of 12 acres (4.8 hectares) with a capacity of 107 million gallons (486 million litres) and a maximum depth of around 72 feet (22m).

Clubbiedean Reservoir is situated next to Torduff Reservoir and a short distance from Bonaly Reservoir. It dates from 1850 and its dimensions are a surface area of 12.8 acres (5.2 hectares), a capacity of 56 million gallons (255 million litres) and a maximum depth of 44 feet (14m).

About two miles (3.2km) to the south-west of this group of three reservoirs lie Harlaw and Threipmuir reservoirs. The latter is the biggest of the reservoirs on the northern edge of the Pentlands. It is also the largest area of fresh water within the City of Edinburgh boundary.

Threipmuir Reservoir occupies an area of what was once marshy ground and may have been the site of a natural loch formed in prehistoric times. At its western end there is still a large area of wetland which attracts wildlife. It has a surface area of 218 acres (88 hectares), and capacity of 518 million gallons (2,359 million litres) but is far shallower than many of the other reservoirs with its maximum depth being around 16 feet (5m). It was created in 1847 by impounding the water of Bavelaw Burn which flowed in a shallow valley. In 1848, Harlaw Reservoir was built immediately below Threipmuir Reservoir, but is of a much smaller size. Its maximum surface area is 30.6 acres (12.4 hectares), with a capacity of 160 million gallons (727 million litres) and depth of around 49 feet (15m). Threipmuir and Harlaw reservoirs were both constructed as compensation reservoirs to ensure that the industries on the Water of Leith did not suffer from water shortages, as many of the springs were being diverted to meet Edinburgh's need for drinking water. Large numbers of Irishmen were employed in the construction of these two reservoirs which were built at the time of the Irish potato famine.

Most of the mills have long since disappeared from the banks of the river but the water from the compensation reservoirs still plays an important role ensuring there is adequate flow the year round for recreational purposes and for wildlife.

There was a proposal in 1845 to construct a reservoir on Salisbury Crags. This project was to have been allowed to proceed providing two fountains, which would hurl water 200 ft (61m), into the air, were constructed in front of Holyrood Palace. Another projected reservoir that was never built was to be situated in York Place on a site now occupied by the Scottish National Portrait Gallery. Its function was to have been to supply Leith with water.

A new reservoir was, however, constructed on Castlehill, next to the Esplanade. It was on the site of the cistern that was constructed to store water from Swanston springs in the mid-eighteenth century. The new Castlehill Reservoir, constructed in 1849, held 1.5 million gallons (6.8 million litres). The depth of the water was around 25 feet (7.6m). It was supplied by Clubbiedean and Moorfoot reservoirs as well as Comiston and Swanston springs, the latter supply ceasing in 1981, a few years before the closure of this storage facility. In its final years this reservoir's main role was to maintain a constant water supply to the taller buildings in Princes Street and George Street. At the end of the twentieth century the tank was drained of water and the building opened as a tourist attraction housing tartan-weaving demonstrations. Even when the reservoir was there few people were aware of its existence. It was enclosed within imposing sandstone walls but had the appearance of a conventional building.

Another reservoir can be found at Alnwickhill Filtration Works, Liberton just over two miles (3.2km) from the city centre. Not many people who pass the entrance of the works are aware of its existence either, despite the fact that it is not enclosed in a building like Castlehill Reservoir. Construction began in 1876 along with a number of filters as part of the Moorfoot scheme. From 1886 water from the Crawley scheme at Glencorse was piped into it as well. The Alnwickhill reservoir, which services filtration works next to it, is about 900 feet (275m) in length and 250 feet wide (76m) with a depth of 22 feet (6.7m) and capacity of 20 million gallons (91 million litres). There was a plan in 1895 to construct a reservoir of a similar size at Fairmilehead but the project remained on the drawing board.

Edinburgh's demand for water had outgrown the capacity of local supplies by the late nineteenth century. In the early years of the twenty-first century water is piped from reservoirs situated in the upper reaches of the Tweed Valley as well as Loch Lomond. The schemes within the current city boundary of Edinburgh in the late twentieth century only met about five per cent of its needs.

A number of ponds and reservoirs have been constructed solely to meet the demand of water for agriculture and industrial uses. A fenced-off pond 30 feet (9 metres) in depth still exists at the corner of Gypsy Brae and West Granton Road. The water was utilised for cooling purposes for the now closed Granton Gasworks. Its warm water was an attraction for wildlife. It is intended to incorporate this pond in the waterfront development scheme planned to regenerate the area over the first decade of the twenty-first century. While most traces of the gasworks will be swept away, the cooling pond is to be remodelled and incoporated in an 8 hectare belt of parkland. At Kirkliston to the west of Edinburgh a pond called Pike's Pool (Alison Park) was created in the nineteenth century to supply the nearby distillery. Humbie Reservior (8 acres/3.2 hectares) was constructed in the same century to supplement this source. Both bodies of water are retained by dams of earth with stone facings. Humbie Reservoir (8 acres/3 hectares) fed Pike's Pool (5 acres/2 hectares) through a tunnel which is large enough for a person to walk through.

Lochrin Distillery, near Tolcross, was in 1817 was the largest distillery in Scotland, and had several large ponds situated close to it. These presumably were used as a source of water for manufacturing processes. Several mills also had sizeable mill ponds according to nineteenth-century maps. One was created by damming the Braidburn and was found just to the south of the old dovecote on Gilmerton Road where there is now a modern housing development. Another was located immediately east of seventeenth-century Peffermill House. It was a long crescent-shaped pond on a site now occupied by industrial units. The pond had gone by the end of the nineteenth century.

In the late eighteenth century and early nineteenth century there was a large number of ponds in the vicinity of Restalrig. At that time most of this area was open countryside and there were numerous orchards here. The ponds were used for irrigation purposes. The largest group of ponds was located just west of Restalrig and some of them were around 200 ft (60m) in length and breadth. They were supplied by the River Tummel which had also been used to create the Nor Loch. A report published in 1862 states that there were 250 acres (101 hectares) of irrigated meadowland at Craigentinny. The Jordan Burn was put to a similar use irrigating about 11 acres (5 hectares). The Lochrin Burn, which had been used for watering fields since at least the sixteenth century, irrigated 90 acres (36 hectares) at Dalry. There was an attempt at irrigation at Claremont Crescent and at an extensive tract of land at Corstorphine. Edinburgh in the mid-nineteenth century was 'surrounded by these artificial swamps and enveloped in their pestilential odours'. Dr Littlejohn expressed the opinion that many deaths in the poorer quarters of the city could be attributed to unhealthy character of the breezes caused by the irrigated fields which were serviced by drains and watercourses containing the city's waste and sewage. The days of this form of irrigation were numbered!

At South Queensferry there is a street called Loch Street. Today there is no sign of any pond or loch in the area but there is a small body of water shown on a 1769 map and an early nineteenth-century map. This pond may have supplied water for irrigation purposes. It occupied an area of now open ground to the north of Inchcolm Terrace and a short distance to the east of the A90 road just before the toll barriers at the Forth Road Bridge. There was a marshy area here at the beginning of the twentieth century. Another small loch or pond once existed a short distance to the east. It was known as Thieve's Loch and is shown on a map dated 1757 but had disappeared by 1800. The name is probably early Scots, derived from Thieves Loch, a loch noted for thorny bushes or brambles along its shores. A road, with the name of Sommerville Gardens near Dalmeny, has been constructed on the site once occupied by this small body of water.

In the nineteenth century a reservoir was constructed near South Queensferry to supply its inhabitants with water. During 1817 Lord

Rosebery became the Provost of the Burgh and resolved to improve its supply of soft water. His property of Niven's Green contained 'a large ravine formed by nature to make one of the completest reservoirs imaginable'. The elevated position of the reservoir made it ideal for supplying the three wells in the town. In 1830 due to a drought the dam was increased in height. Niven's Green Park was constructed on the site of the reservoir.

Flooded Quarry Workings

ONE UNINTENTIONAL RESULT of the quarrying of stone in the vicinity of Edinburgh has been the creation of numerous ponds in the vacated workings. While many of them have had a limited lifespan a handful have become long-term features of the landscape. The flooded workings have been put to a number of uses including some of a sinister nature.

In 1530 a Marione Clerk was convicted for concealing her infection during an outbreak of the plague, going to mass on Sunday and endangering the inhabitants of Edinburgh. She was sentenced to be drowned at Quarrel (Quarry) Holes located outside Greyfriars Port. Another unfortunate woman called Catherine Heriot was condemned to a similar fate for 'bringing contagious sickness from Leith to Edinburgh' as well as theft. The site of these quarry workings was close to the Burgh Loch but the town authorities obviously avoided using the water of the loch for fear of polluting it by those infected with the plague.

Another source of building materials was on the north-eastern edge of Calton Hill, the workings here going by the name of Upper and Lower Quarry Holes. Many of them were already abandoned by the seventeenth century. There were numerous requests by the Town Council to have them filled in because of the danger they represented. Most of the landowners disregarded such requests, despite the fact that people often fell into the flooded workings and were drowned. In 1691 an Englishman, Lt Byron, was drowned at Nether Quarry Holes, close to where Easter Road is located today. Many of the sources of stone for medieval Edinburgh came from small quarries scattered around the Burgh Muir and particularly on the site of Bruntsfield Links. Another early source of stone for the capital was the Ravelston Quarries. These supplied stone for Holyrood Palace and St Giles Cathedral. Unlike most of the early quarry workings, which have been filled in and built on, several of these survive including one which had a small pond until the end of the twentieth century. This old working is located next to Ravelston Park and east of Ravelston Dykes Road, and in the late nineteenth century was a home to a large pool.

The building of the New Town of Edinburgh created a huge demand for sandstone, much of which came from Craigleith Quarry, a short distance to the east of Ravelston. Unfortunately little trace of this working is visible, with a supermarket standing on part of the site. It was situated on the north side of the junction of Queensferry Road and Craigleith Road. Even when the quarry was in operation, it was partially flooded as shown by a painting of it by James Skene in 1837. At first a water pump driven by a horse was used. In the latter part of the nineteenth century steam engines were employed to try and keep the water at bay. By this time the hole had reached a depth of 350 ft (107m). During much of the twentieth century the quarry was unused and hosted a large pond until it was reclaimed in the 1970s.

Maidencraig Quarry existed a short distance to the west of Craigleith Quarry, on the north side of Queensferry Road. The site is now occupied by a large block of flats of the same name. In the mid-nineteenth century the quarry had fallen into disuse and was filled with a large pool of water. It was reclaimed in the early part of the twentieth century. Another source of stone was Barton Park Quarry, which is now a flooded working, situated in the middle of Bruntsfield Golf Course.

At the very edge of the City of Edinburgh boundary, to the north of Kirkliston, lies Humbie Quarry. It supplied stone for Surgeons' Hall and the Robert Burns Monument but was abandoned in 1868 and became flooded. It has survived in this state until the beginning of the twenty-first century. The flooded quarry has steep sides and is potentially dangerous to anyone visiting the site.

Like Barton Park Quarry, several other flooded workings have been landscaped and converted into attractive landscape features. As early as the beginning of the nineteenth century some of the abandoned quarry workings had their banks planted with trees.

The pond in the grounds of Lauriston Castle was created at the beginning of the twentieth century from a quarry said to have been the source of building material for the original tower house. Due to the problems with the water supply, the pond was considerably reduced in size in 1950. An island in the pond has been planted with rhododendron hybrids.

The disused Granton Gasworks Reservoir is located on the site of a former sandstone quarry. Flooded quarry workings also acted as temporary reservoirs for drinking water in the past. The year 1814 was very dry and the scarcity of water was so great that the magistrates of Edinburgh sent carts to be filled with water from an old working located where Hillside Crescent now stands. Further back in time at the end of the sixteenth century, the Society of Brewers was given permission to boost the supply of available water in the Burgh Loch by laying pipes from water-filled quarries on Bruntsfield Links to the Burgh Loch a short distance below them. Quarries are particularly prone to flooding because the excavations often strike springs of water.

Finally Mortonhall Golf Course, like Bruntsfield Golf Course, has a pond on it, although it is not in an old quarry working. Elf Loch is the name of this small body of water that lies at the southern tip of the Braid Hills. Its name originally referred to a small pond on the top of the Braid Hills, now known as Deidman's Pool. In a description written in 1786 there is mention of a hollow on the south side of the hills of Braid, called Eve's or Elf's Kirk, with a 'pretty natural pond'. The name of Elf Loch may, unfortunately, come from an early name for hill rather than with any connection to the Fairy Kingdom.

Changes in Edinburgh's Coastline

IT IS PROJECTED that global warming could increase the sea levels around the coast of Britain by about 2 ft (0.6m) by 2050. The prospect of such a rise has caused alarm in many quarters as the higher sea levels could flood houses located near the coast and cause disruption to transport and industry. It has been a long-standing belief that the level of the sea around the coast of Scotland has not been subject to change but nothing could be further from the truth.

Going far back in time to around 350 million years ago, the area on which Edinburgh is situated resembled today's American Gulf Coast, with a flat tropical shore consisting of tree-fringed lagoons. The dry land was devoid of any hills. During this epoch central Scotland experienced a dramatic change with the eruption of several volcanoes including Arthur's Seat. When this volcano was active around 325 million years ago, most of it was immersed in the waters of a sea that surrounded it. Only the vent protruded above the waves and at that time Arthur's Seat was twice as high as it is now!

From about 250 million years to two million years ago the Edinburgh area was mainly dry land, with mountains dissected by large rivers that flowed east into seas located on the site of today's North Sea.

In the last two million years, the Edinburgh area was repeatedly buried under hundreds of feet of frozen water in the form of glaciers. The last glaciers melted just 15,000 years ago which is very recent in the timespan of the Earth's history. Around this time, when much water was locked up in the form of ice, neither the Firth of Forth nor the North Sea existed. It was possible to walk eastwards from Edinburgh across dry land bisected by large rivers to Continental Europe. When the glaciers melted they left behind huge amounts of water which formed lochs and large rivers. The process of glaciation, however, destroyed all evidence of the lochs and ponds that existed prior to this cold spell. It is unlikely that much will ever be known about the lochs present in the Edinburgh area tens of thousands of years ago.

Around the same time as the prehistoric lochs were being formed, the sea on the shoreline of the Edinburgh area was rising – 12,000 years ago the sea level was a staggering 130 feet (40m) above the present level. The sea reached as far inland as Holyrood Abbey and lapped round the foot of Calton Hill. The edge of the seashore also extended to the foot of the New Town and waves would have been breaking over much of Stockbridge and Canonmills. This also must have resulted in the sites of some of the prehistoric lochs such as Lochend, Canonmills and Holyrood being initially filled with salt water. The sea levels then began to drop, reaching a similar level to that of today around 9,000 years ago. The levels then rose again reaching a maximum of about 32 feet (10m) above the current level around 6,000 years ago. Areas such as the site of the promenade at Portobello and Leith Links were submerged by the sea. The water then retreated again until it reached its present position.

One direct consequence on the shape of the coastline caused by the activities of man occurred in October 1855. There was a large quarry at Granton Point covering 8 acres (3 hectares) which the sea flooded to within ten minutes of breaking through the barrier that had previously kept its waters at bay. The quarry was abandoned after this disaster.

Although rising sea levels caused by global warming may in future cause all sorts of disruption, they do not generally pose an immediate threat to life and property on the coast of Edinburgh. Tidal waves, however, strike with little warning and give little time for those living near the coast to escape. It was thought that Scotland did not suffer from this form of natural hazard but recent evidence has proved otherwise. Around 8,000 years ago, the east coast of Scotland, including the Edinburgh area, was struck by a large tidal wave, estimated to have been at least 30 feet (10 metres) and possibly as much as 100 feet (30 metres) in height. This natural disaster was triggered by a massive marine landslide occurring on the continental slope off Storegga, south-west Norway. Although the height of the waves generated by the movement may not have been much higher than the greatest storm waves, they would have travelled much faster and involved much greater energy. The water of this tidal wave may have travelled a considerable distance inland from the coast, flooding the ground now occupied by the low-lying parts of Edinburgh. The mesolithic hunter-gatherer communities may have been overwhelmed by this natural hazard. For those that were not drowned it certainly would have left its mark on the minds of those who witnessed it. This phenomenon affected most of the east coast of Scotland as a silty clay deposited by the tidal wave has been found from Dunbar to Inverness and as far inland as Stirling. Excavations in the centre of Inverness have uncovered evidence that a primitive human settlement was wiped out by the enormous wave. Silt deposits were found beside evidence of a human dwelling, including charcoal from a makeshift fire. It is thought that Inverness was at least 18 feet (5.5 metres) underwater for around three days. Five massive waves battered the area before the water subsided. The coastline in the vicinity of Edinburgh may well have suffered in a similar manner.

It has been suggested by scientists that an undersea earthquake or a massive release of methane gas in the North Sea could again trigger a tidal wave of this size some time in the future. This would have devastating results for Edinburgh, the floodwater probably recreating many of the long-lost lochs once found here.

APPENDIX X

The Wellhouse Tower

Introduction

SITUATED UNDER the north face of the Castle rock, in a place which the sun's rays barely reach, can be found the fragmented remains of the Wellhouse Tower. Although it was a modest building its loss to hostile forces could determine the fate of Edinburgh Castle and in turn the course of Scottish history.

The Castle appears to occupy an impregnable site on top of an outcrop of volcanic rock. Ironically the same rock that made the fortifications nearly inaccessible to hostile armies was also responsible for creating an Achilles Heel in its defences. The volcanic basalt on which the Castle was perched had very poor water retaining properties. When it rained

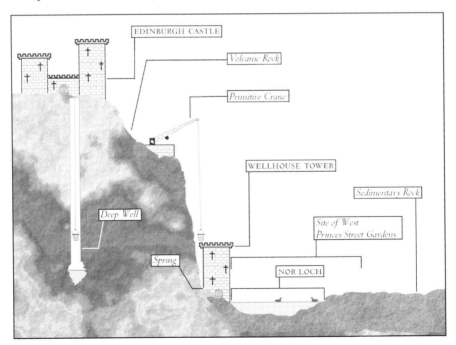

View of the Well House Tower drawn by James Skene in 1818. He was responsible for carrying out the reclamation of the bed of the Nor Loch enabling the site to be eventually transformed into West Princes Street Gardens. Fortunately he was also interested in archaeology and he recorded many of the finds he made in the mud-filled valley. (*By courtesy of Edinburgh City Libraries.*)

water would very rapidly run down the rock and emerge as springs at its base. Thus there was little water available for the garrison of the Castle on the summit of the rock. It was where one of the springs emerged at the foot of the volcanic basalt that the Wellhouse was constructed in the fourteenth century.

Construction of the Wellhouse Tower

PRIOR TO THE BUILDING of the Wellhouse Tower, the medieval Castle was supplied by a deep well sunk some 90 feet (27 metres) into the basalt rock. Water only accumulated at this point, on the east side of the hill, because there the volcanic rock came into contact with a more porous rock, namely sandstone. This water-retaining rock forms most of the ground on which the Castle esplanade is built. Unfortunately this well, known as the Fore Well, would sometimes dry up when the demand for water was high. Hugo Arnot, writing in the eighteenth century, said the following about this water supply: 'The water which is very bad, served in scanty supply by a well upwards of a hundred feet and in the event of a siege, the concussion of the rock, by the continued discharge of artillery makes the water subside.' Over the centuries the site around the well became filled in with rubble as old buildings were replaced, hence the apparent increase in depth of the Fore Well from 90 feet (27 metres) to around 100 feet (30 metres) in the later centuries.

When Edinburgh Castle was captured from the English in 1314 by the forces of the Scottish King Robert the Bruce, the structure was demolished to prevent it from being used by hostile forces. In the process of razing the building to the ground the Fore Well was blocked and its location was lost for several decades. Between 1335 and 1379, when the Castle rock was again used as a fortification, the garrison was entirely dependent on a spring found at the base of the cliffs. This was a very unsatisfactory arrangement particularly if the Castle was attacked, as its water supply was outside its main defensive walls.

In the years of 1361 and 1362, the Wellhouse Tower was built at the foot of the north side of the Castle rock to secure the water supply from one of the larger springs. It apparently was built by Robert Hog, a resident of Edinburgh who was high in King David II's favour. First a new well was constructed and the following year the Tower was built to enclose it.

The Role of the Wellhouse Tower

ALTHOUGH THE WELLHOUSE TOWER was a modest structure, being little more than a square tower, it occupied a key position in the Castle's defences. In 1312–13, a small party of around thirty men led by William Francis ascended the cliff on the north side of the hill and scaled the outer walls with the assistance of ladders. They opened the Castle gates and the English defenders were put to the sword. It is thought that the starting point for the party that scaled the cliffs was close to where the Wellhouse Tower is found today. Perhaps with this event still fresh in the minds of the garrison, it was decided that the Castle should not fall to such audacious attack again and the Tower was one consequence of this event. In addition to guarding this part of the Castle rock, the Tower acted as a defensive gateway for the outer defences. The north side of Castlehill, which now forms part of West Princes Street Gardens, is thought to have been enclosed by an earthen wall in the early part of the fourteenth century to form the outer ward of Edinburgh Castle. Around the same time as the Wellhouse Tower was constructed the earthen wall was replaced by one made of stone.

There is thought to have long been an ancient pathway along the northern edge of the Castle rock. The Wellhouse Tower was constructed a few feet away from the cliff leaving room for a narrow passageway between it and the building. Horses for the Castle were kept in the vicinity of the present day King's Stables Road. They may have passed through the gate at the Wellhouse Tower when being taken to the knights

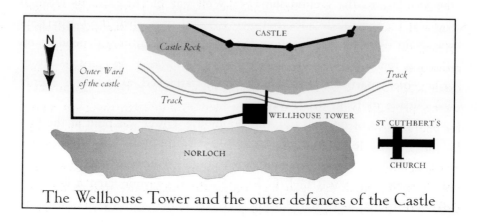

The Wellhouse Tower and the outer defences of the Castle

garrisoned within the fortress as they prepared for battle. Maitland, one of Edinburgh's earliest historians, gives further evidence of the defensive role of the Tower: '... and without the said Tower, to the Westward, at the Distance of about eighty yards seems to have been an Outwork, by the Remains of a strong stonern Wall adjoining to the Castle rock'. It is thought that this may have been part of the defences to the gateway at the Wellhouse Tower designed to narrow the approach to the entrance.

To the east of the Wellhouse Tower are the remains of a stone wall that once formed part of the medieval City Wall of Edinburgh. It ran some 850 feet (225 metres) in an easterly direction from the Tower before turning south and crossing the Castlehill. On the north side of the Tower and its adjoining wall was the Nor Loch. Before the formation of the loch the River Tummel flowed through the low ground on the north side of the Castle. It is possible that the Wellhouse Tower was built in conjunction with the creation of the loch. Certainly the spring from here is said to have been one of its main sources of water for it. When the Nor Loch was formed its waters lapped around the foot of the Tower. This would have limited the access to the gate in this building to a narrow pathway at the base of the rock. Thus the Wellhouse Tower should not be regarded in isolation as a defensive feature but having a key role in conjunction with the other main protective elements, namely the Nor Loch and Town Walls. Long after the outer ward of the Castle disappeared, the ground remained under the control of the Castle. In fact the land on this side of Princes Street Gardens still belongs to the Crown, a legacy dating back to the fourteenth century when it was part of the outer defences of the fortress.

Finally it should be mentioned that the Wellhouse Tower was the major source of water for the garrison from 1362 to 1381. When war with England threatened in 1381, a search was made for the Fore Well which was rediscovered and brought back into use. Prior to that water had to be carried up to the top of the hill from the Wellhouse Tower. Even after the re-opening of the Fore Well it remained an important source of water for the garrison. It should be noted that water was not generally drunk by the soldiers in the Castle but was used for the brewing of ale. Wine was generally drunk by the knights and the nobility. During the siege of 1689 it is recorded that two bombs hit the storehouse destroying the defenders' supply of ale and forcing the soldiers to drink water until more ale was brewed! Knights, however, required large quantities of water for their horses. A horse consumed around 10 gallons (45 litres) of water a day. When Edinburgh Castle was occupied by English forces in the year 1299–1300, the garrison numbered 347 with 156 horses. Water was required also for fighting fires which even in peacetime occurred fairly frequently as many buildings were made of wood with thatched roofs.

Above the Wellhouse Tower, the foundations of a square platform structure can be seen perched at the edge of the cliff. This is known as Wallace's Cradle. The Wellhouse Tower in early accounts was sometimes referred to as Wallace's Tower. The platform also goes by another name, the Crane Bastion, which gives a clue to its possible role. It is thought that a wooden crane or hoist was mounted on the platform to lift containers of water up to the Castle, to avoid water having to be transported by hand up a steep and narrow path. As the Wellhouse Tower also played a significant role in the defence of Edinburgh Castle it is suggested that Wallace's Cradle may have been built to enhance this function. Being located on the edge of a steep precipice it would have been an ideal site for dropping rocks and other missiles on hostile forces trying to enter the Castle through the gate at the Wellhouse Tower or attempting to capture the water supply. There is unfortunately no record as to which role this structure was utilised for.

Early History of the Wellhouse Tower

LIKE WALLACE'S CRADLE mentioned above, little is known of the events experienced by this solitary tower in the Middle Ages. The first mention of the Tower while under siege occurs in the sixteenth century. The Castle was being held in the name of Mary Queen of Scots against government forces, who later were assisted by troops sent by Queen Elizabeth I of England. During the years of 1572–73, the fortifications on the rock underwent a vicious bombardment by large siege guns. At first Edinburgh Castle successfully held out against the attackers but during the early months of 1573 the bombardment became more intense and the water supply began to run low. The main well on top of the Castle rock became choked with rubble as the massive towers which crowned the summit were smashed by the besiegers' cannon. The garrison then had to rely on water from springs at the foot of the rock but due to the close proximity of the enemy the collection of water was a hazardous enterprise. A contemporary account states that on 16 May cannon opened fire on Wallace's Tower, which contained the iron gate that protected one of the Castle's entrances. The bombardment then continued intermittently until 21 May. In fact one of the gun batteries was on the north side of the Nor Loch directly opposite the Wellhouse Tower. The structure appears to have been left undefended for much of the siege as there is no mention of it being garrisoned in either English or Scottish accounts. It could be assumed that Kirkcaldy of Grange had considered the site undefendable. Also there is no record in old Treasury Records of cannon being supplied for the Tower. At the end of the siege the building is said to have been left extensively damaged and was never repaired. Much of the rest of the Castle suffered the same fate and had to be totally rebuilt.

When the Castle was rebuilt after the siege, priority was given to finding another source of water on top of the rock and eventually a second well was dug on its western side inside the defensive walls. There were several attacks on Edinburgh Castle in the following century although none compared with the severity of that of 1572–73.

The last siege of the Castle took place in 1689 when the Duke of Gordon held the fortress in the name of the deposed King James VII. The route down the north side of the rock to the Wellhouse Tower seems to have been utilised as a route for sending out spies long after the other exits had been blocked up by the besiegers. The garrison, although relatively small in number appears to have been short of water as there was a fall of snow, rather unusual in May, and soldiers gathered up the snow to put it into their drinking vessels for fear that the wells would fail. There is evidence that the Wellhouse Tower was manned for at least some of the time as it is recorded in a contemporary account that when a party of besiegers looked as if they were going to intercept a Mr Ross who was attempting to enter the Castle, they were scared off by the appearance of two soldiers in the building. By the summer of that year the garrison surrendered after sustaining minimal losses.

Even as late as 1755, the general in charge of Edinburgh Castle complained that what was most needed was a decent water supply and money spent on further improving the fortifications would be wasted if this problem was not rectified. In fact the ruined Wellhouse Tower continued to be used by the soldiers of Edinburgh Castle as an additional source of water up to 1821.

Recent History

BY THE NINTEENTH CENTURY, the Nor Loch had disappeared and the valley floor along with the Castlehill was converted into a private garden for the owners of the newly constructed houses in Princes Street. James Skene was responsible for converting the marshy ground into landscaped gardens. He also had an interest in archaeology and carried out what is thought to have been the only excavation based around the Wellhouse Tower to the present time. What he found was actually something of a disappointment to him. Nonetheless he made some interesting finds, which included several coins predating the building of the Wellhouse. This is an indication that the springs here may well have been in use before the 1360s and the coins may have been dropped by someone refreshing theirselves from its waters. Among the coins found around the site of the Tower included one possibly from the reign of Edward I, several from Edward III and a numerous collection from the time of Oliver Cromwell and the Civil War in the mid-seventeenth century. Rather surprisingly several foreign coins were also unearthed. James Skene observed that silver pennies of King Edward's reign were the most frequently found coins in Scotland. They were used to pay English troops fighting the Scots and were sent in great numbers from the south.

A more gruesome discovery came in the form of a thick human skull which had shattered into many pieces. It was found at the foot of the stairway which once gave access to a ladder and the upper storey of the Wellhouse Tower. It is thought to be part of the body of some unfortunate who fell down the stairs, smashing his head at the bottom.

Many fragments of bomb shells were dug up around the ruined tower. A 48 pound (22 kilograms) shell was found embedded in the Wellhouse Tower's wall by James Skene. The position of the ball in the wall indicated that it had been fired from a position where Regent Morton had sited one of his gun batteries in the siege of 1572–73. In later centuries the general practice was to use lighter cannonballs weighing around 24 pounds (11 kilograms). The continual battering of a target by such ammunition had in fact a more devastating effect than the occasional strike by the 48 pound ball which seemed to have been favoured by the sixteenth-century attackers of Edinburgh Castle.

The Restoration of the Well

WHEN PRINCES STREET GARDENS were created in the early years of the nineteenth century, access was restricted to owners of neighbouring properties who had keys to the gates. As the century progressed the public were allowed in with increasing regularity for special occasions such as performances by military bands. In 1872 the clerk for the Gardens received a letter from Captain Alexander of the 93rd Sutherland Highlanders stationed in Edinburgh Castle, proposing that a bandstand should be erected. A further letter from the same officer made the additional suggestion that the Wellhouse Tower should be restored. This would be financed from performances given in the Royal Theatre. The officers in army units stationed in Edinburgh apparently often participated in these shows! In addition it was also proposed to put up a drinking fountain at the Wellhouse Tower in place of the wooden pump then used for drawing water.

It was envisaged that the walls of the Tower would be restored and roofed in. James Drummond was asked to provide drawings of how the Wellhouse Tower originally looked based on old prints of the Nor Loch. A Mr Gowans offered to carry out the restoration work free of charge, except for the cost of the building materials. Unfortunately the restoration work never commenced and the Tower was allowed to continue to decay, resulting in the shambolic ruin that is visible today. The old fashioned pump, however, was replaced by a simple receptacle of grey granite from which two jets of water emerged. The fountain was designed by James Drummond, RSA. The work for the new fountain was carried out for a total cost of £64. The money was raised by the 93rd Highlanders who are commemorated on the plaque at the fountain which bears the following inscription on a sandstone slab:

St Margaret's Well. The fountain of the ancient Wellhouse Tower celebrated in the history of the Castle since the time of St Margaret, Queen of Scotland in the 11th century. Restored by the officers of the 93rd Sutherland Highlanders. AD 1873.

In addition to the description there are also carved the arms of Malcolm Canmore, Queen Margaret's husband and above that an old Scottish

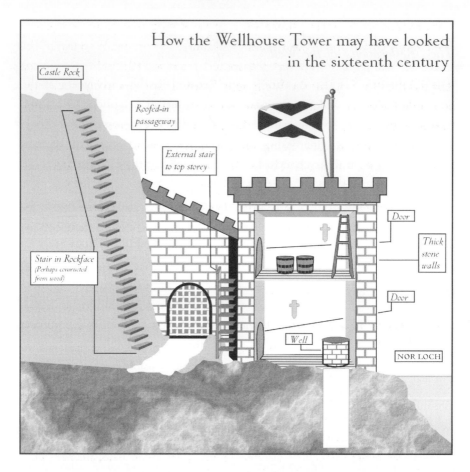

How the Wellhouse Tower may have looked in the sixteenth century

Castle Rock

Roofed-in passageway

External stair to top storey

Stair in Rockface
(Perhaps constructed from wood)

Door

Thick stone walls

Door

Well

NOR LOCH

crown. The fountain continued to be used until the early years of the twentieth century. It seems to have been no longer functional by the 1930s.

Although the ruin is often referred to as St Margaret's Well and is backed up by the fact that the plaque at this site also carries her name, there is some doubt that it is the original well.

Most historians now believe that the St Margaret's Well referred to in documents of the early Middle Ages was situated on the west side of the Castle rock, close to where King's Stables Road is today. The first reference to a well in the vicinity of the Castle rock occurs in a document recording the donation of land 'under the Castle from the fountain which rises close to the King's Garden and along the road leading to the church'. King David I gifted this land around 1127 to the newly founded Abbey at Holyrood.

Historians in Victorian times were in no doubt that Saint Margaret's Well was located where the ruined Wellhouse Tower stands today. If the name St Margaret's Well was transposed from a little well to a spring that fed the Nor Loch at the Wellhouse Tower, it appears to have occurred at a relatively early date. In some accounts of the siege of Edinburgh Castle in the years of 1572–73, St Margaret's Well is referred to by name and the description of it being on the north side of the rock fits the location of the Wellhouse Tower. It should finally be noted that this St Margaret's Well should not be confused with another well of the same name that was located at Restalrig. The stonework from this well was transported to Holyrood Park in 1859 where it was rebuilt and can be viewed today.

The Wellhouse Tower

JAMES SKENE, who excavated the ruin in the early nineteenth century, wrote the following description of the fortification:

> The removal of rubbish instead of revealing the expected well brought a covered way to light leading along the southern wall of the Tower to a strongly fortified doorway, opening outside, of the purpose of which as a sally port or posterngate there could be little doubt from the defences of the tower being principally directed to this point. The walls are here of very great strength, penetrated in the middle of the solid mass by a square cavity for the reception of a beam which slid across the inside of the door for its protection and in case of the door being driven in the inside to protect the covered way. The port opens out to a chasm in the rock about twenty feet in width, [7 metres], over which when occasion required a gangway or drawbridge was most likely thrust and here the purpose of the building placed on the ledge of rock above [referring to Wallace's Cradle] becomes exceedingly obvious, occupying an admirable position for the defences of this assailable point.
>
> In constructing a path within these few days which required the removal of a considerable bank from the foot of the rock, some very obvious indications have been uncovered of the communication between the under and upper tower, by means of a scrambling stair, constructed in such tortuous direction as the projections of the rock would permit and directed

towards a natural fissure in the cliff, where a ladder might have been conveniently accomplished to give access to the building above. The remains of this stair were covered with earth and rubbish to the depth of eight or ten feet.

Today the most significant part of the structure still standing is that of the east wall. Not much else remains. The Wellhouse Tower was rectangular in shape, although verging towards a square 38 feet long (13 metres) and 30 feet broad (10 metres). There was, however, a wing on the north east corner of the building which is thought to have contained the well. On the south east corner there was another similar projection whose function was to give access from the upper storey across the covered entrance. Most of the Wellhouse Tower was built of stone taken from the adjoining cliffs. Some sandstone was used for the walls in addition to the volcanic rock. On the southern wall two narrow windows survive which originally looked onto the covered passageway which gave access to the outer defences of Edinburgh Castle.

The Wellhouse Tower is thought to have been guarded by two circular stone bastions (pentagonal projections from a fortification) the remains of which can still be seen today close to the ruin). They are still attached to a portion of the Medieval City Wall which enclosed much of early Edinburgh. It can be seen extending a short distance to the east of the Tower. To the north of it lay the waters of the Nor Loch before it was drained.

Despite the rather humble remains of the Wellhouse Tower on view today it should be remembered that it predates most of the buildings in Edinburgh Castle. It is a reminder of a far older Castle dating back to the Middle Ages which was totally different in appearance to the present fortification. Finally the Wellhouse Tower also has the distinction of being the lowest structure of Edinburgh Castle, due to its position on the valley floor.

Bibliography

WHILE RESEARCHING THE HISTORY of the Nor Loch numerous books and journals on Edinburgh were consulted. Many were found to contain no information on the loch while others, including several well-known accounts of the history of the city, dismiss the subject in no more than a paragraph. The most useful source of material was the extracts of the Records of the Burgh of Edinburgh published in the twentieth century. The several volumes cover a period of about three centuries, from the mid-fifteenth century to the early eighteenth century which just about coincides with the later history of the loch and its reclamation. There are numerous references to the loch, usually in association with matters concerning land disputes or the provision of slaughterhouses on its banks. Other than the original records, perhaps the most useful source of information was a series of articles entitled 'The legends of the Nor Loch' which appeared in the *Scotsman* newspaper in 1898. The author, who unfortunately is not credited in the newspaper, appears to have actually based his research on the original city records and not just plagiarised text from earlier histories of Edinburgh. At the end of his series of articles the author suggested that the topic of the Nor Loch would make a suitable subject for a book! There is also a reference to the fact that many of the city records had been destroyed, first through military conflict and in later centuries due to carelessness. Thus perhaps many events and incidents that took place on the Nor Loch are now lost in the mists of time. The author's articles seem not to have fared much better, being totally lost in the archives of the library and not mentioned in any bibliographies or references. They were only found by chance in a newspaper cuttings file donated many years ago to the main reference library.

The best-known source of information on the Nor Loch is contained in an extensive chapter in a book entitled *Castle and Town* by D. Robertson, published in 1928. Although there is no bibliography, much information that appeared in 'The Legends of the Nor Loch' articles is also repeated in it. The sequel volume, *The Princes Street Proprietors*, contains an extensive account of the later history of the valley detailing the draining of the loch and the numerous land disputes that arose with its reclamation. An account of one such dispute between the City of Edinburgh and the Royal Ordnance, who were responsible for Edinburgh Castle, is contained in the records of the Court of Session. This court case also contains several references to the area covered by the Nor Loch when it existed. One of the best books in recent years is *Edinburgh in Olden Times* by Duncan Fraser (1976) which paints a graphic picture of life and events in the City of Edinburgh when the loch formed its northern boundary. The first histories of Edinburgh appeared at the end of the eighteenth century and were written by persons who would have first-hand experience of the loch. Thus it is rather surprising there were not more references made to it in these early accounts of the city's past.

Books

Adams, Ian H. (1978), *The Making of Urban Scotland*, London: Croom Helm.

Arnot, Hugo (1779), *History of Edinburgh*, T. Longman and T. Cadell; W. Creech, London: Edinburgh.

Barclay, John Bruce (1965), *Edinburgh from the Earliest Times to the Present Day*, London: A & C Black Ltd.

Birrell, J. F. (1980), *An Edinburgh Alphabet*, Edinburgh: Mercat Press.

Butler, Rev. D., MA (1906), *The Tron Kirk of Edinburgh or Christ's Kirk at the Tron – A History*, Oliphant, Edinburgh: Anderson & Ferrier.

Chambers, Robert (1868), *The Traditions of Edinburgh*, Edinburgh & London: W & R Chambers Ltd.

Cockburn, Henry (1910), *Memorials of His Time*, New Edition, Edinburgh: T.N. Foulis.

Fletcher, Harold & Brown, W., *The Royal Botanic Gardens, Edinburgh, 1670–1970*, HMSO Edinburgh.

Fraser, Duncan (1976), *Edinburgh in Olden Times*, Montrose: Standard Press.

Gifford, J., McWilliam, C. & Walker, D. (1984), *Edinburgh – The Buildings of Scotland*, Harmondsworth, Middlesex: Penguin Books.

Grant, J. (1880) *Old and New Edinburgh*, 3 volumes, London: Cassell.

Gray, W. Forbes (1925), *An Edinburgh Miscellany*, Edinburgh: Robert Grant & Son

Harris, Stuart (1996), The Place Names of Edinburgh, Edinburgh: Gordon Wright Publishing Ltd.

Lorimer, George (1915), *The Early Days of St Cuthbert's Church*, Edinburgh and London: William Blackwood & Sons.

Lynch, Michael (1981), *Edinburgh and the Reformation*, Edinburgh: John Donald.

Malcolm, C.A. (1938), *Princes Street – a History of the Life Association of Scotland*, The Life Association of Scotland.

Robertson, D. (1935), *The Princes Street Proprietors*, Edinburgh & London: Oliver and Boyd.

—, and Wood, M., (1928), *Castle and Town*, Chapters in the History of the Royal Burgh of Edinburgh, Edinburgh: Oliver and Boyd.

—, and others (1929), *Edinburgh 1329–1929*, Edinburgh: Oliver & Boyd.

Royal Commission on the Ancient Monuments (1951), *An Inventory of the Ancient and Historical Monuments of the City of Edinburgh*, HMSO.

Royal Scottish Geographical Society (1919), *The Early Views and Maps of Edinburgh 1544 to 1852*.

Scottish Burgh Records Society, *Extracts from the Records of the Burgh of Edinburgh 1403–1528*. Also subsequent volumes of Extracts of the Burgh of Edinburgh Records covering the period up to c.1720.

Smith, J.S. (1890), *The Grange of St Giles. The Bass and Other Baronial Homes of the Dick Lauder Family*, Edinburgh: T.A. Constable.

Smith, Jane Stewart (1924), *Historic Stones and Stories of Bygone Edinburgh*, Edinburgh: Constable.

Youngston, A.J. (1968), *The Making of Classical Edinburgh*, Edinburgh: Edinburgh University Press.

Journals

THE BOOK OF THE OLD EDINBURGH CLUB

Angus, William (1913), 'The Incorporated Trade of the Skinners of Edinburgh', vol 6.

Anon, (1928), 'The Siege of the Edinburgh Castle, 1689', vol 16.

Bryce, Moir (1912), 'Saint Margaret and her Chapel in Edinburgh', vol 5.

Butchart, R. (1962), 'Lost Opportunities, Nor Loch', vol 31.

Cowan, William (1924), 'Bearford's Parks', vol 13.

Kerr, Henry (1930), 'Gabriel's and Other Old Roads', vol 17.

Malcolm, C.A. (1925), 'The Gardens of the Castle', vol 14.

— (1928), 'The Diary of John Nicoll', vol 16.

THE SCOTSMAN

Anon (1898), 'Legends of the North Loch', 15 January, 22 January, 4 February.

— (1988), 'The Growing Pains of the Gardens', 13 August.

THE EVENING NEWS (EDINBURGH)

Anon (1987), 'The Capital's Forgotten Loch', 18 April.

Brown, Neil (1988), 'Looking at Auld Reekie from the Parapets', 17 September.

Dunlop, Jean (1965), 'And On That Grass Bold Knights Have Battled It Out', 16 October.

Mackay, John (1986), 'Now Edinburgh Begins to Take Shape (the Growth of the City)', 2 August.

Vass, John (1985), 'From Evil Marsh to a Rural Haven'.

TRANSACTIONS OF THE SOCIETY OF THE ANTIQUARIES OF SCOTLAND

Millar, Peter, 'Was the Town of Edinburgh an Open and Defenceless One Previous to 1450?' vol 9, 1886–87, New Series.

Skene, James, 'The Well House Tower', vol 2, 1831, second edition.

Other Journals

Horsburgh, W.M., 'The Nor Loch', *Edinburgh Today*, vol 6.

Tait, D. (1945), 'Geological Notes on (a) The Nor Loch, and (b) The Fore Well in Edinburgh Castle', *Transactions of the Edinburgh Geological Society*, vol 14, part I.

Sources for Prehistoric Lochs

The section on the prehistoric lochs of Edinburgh was based on the following articles:

Bennie, James, *Ancient Lakes of Edinburgh*.

'Geological Survey of Scotland', in the *Proceedings of the Royal Physical Society*, c. 1890.

Cadell, Henry, 'Some Ancient Landmarks of Midlothian', *The Scottish Geographical Magazine*, Edinburgh, Constable, 1893.

Other sources included Historical and Geological maps of Edinburgh, newspaper cuttings and information from local history books.